Growing and Flourishing

Growing and Flourishing

The Ecology of Church Growth

Stephen Spencer

with Mwita Akiri

scm press

© Stephen Spencer, 2019

First published in 2019 by the SCM Press Norwich
Editorial office
3rd Floor, Invicta House
108–114 Golden Lane
London EC1Y OTG, UK

www.scmpress.co.uk

SCM Press is an imprint of Hymns Ancient & Modern Ltd
(a registered charity)

Hymns Ancient & Modern® is a registered trademark of
Hymns Ancient & Modern Ltd
13A Hellesdon Park Road, Norwich,
Norfolk NR6 5DR, UK

British Library Cataloguing in Publication data

A catalogue record for this book is available
from the British Library

978 0 334 05734 5

Typeset by Regent Typesetting Ltd
Printed and bound in Great Britain by
CPI Group (UK) Ltd

Contents

Preface

This book has grown from friendship with some generous and committed people and whatever is of merit in these pages is due to them. First of all, friends in the Anglican Church of Tanzania, in Mara Region, provided the inspiration and insight to launch this study. Among them must be mentioned Bishop Hilkiah Omindo of Mara Diocese (now retired) and his wife Martha, Bishop Mwita Akiri of Tarime Diocese (who has generously contributed text to this book), Lay Canon Arthur Mauya, the untiring Mara diocesan link officer, Melina Galibona, the assistant link officer, Salome Polycarp and the Revd Charles Mwita, the link officers for Tarime Diocese, the Revd Peter Oyoo, the link officer for Rorya Diocese, Canon Gaspar Kassanda, the director of evangelism for Mara Diocese, and Canon Moses Yamo, the principal of Bunda Bible College.

In Wakefield Diocese, which became part of the combined Leeds Diocese in 2014, I am immensely grateful to all of those involved in supporting the link with Tanzania and in helping it to grow and flourish, especially Bishop Stephen Platten, who invited me to become the Link Officer and described the diocesan link with Mara as 'the jewel in the crown' of the diocese, and Oriel Kelly, Canon Michael Storey, Sally Firth, Edwina Offori, Bishop Tony Robinson, Canon Maggie McLean, Angela Byram and Bishop Nick Baines for their support and encouragement.

The later chapters of this book also draw on four years of fulfilling ministry at St Martin's Church, Brighouse and St John's Church, Clifton in the Diocese of Wakefield/Leeds. I am very grateful to the people of these churches for their support and commitment to ministry, especially the Revd Michelle

Petch, the Revd Andrew Hall, Tony and Sue Empson, Rachel and Steve Acheson, Alan and Deirdre Sparks, Gail Crisp, Don Bickerton, Helen Lever, Mike and Judi Taylor, the late Debbie Spivey, Graham Stanley and the staff and children at St Andrew's Church of England primary schools and St John's Academy.

The forming of experience and insights into a connected and coherent essay depends on there being an audience willing to listen and engage with it. For this I am grateful to students and colleagues of St Hild College, Mirfield (previously the Yorkshire Ministry Course) who have done just this. Thanks are especially due to the principal, Canon Mark Powley, who invited me to lead a session at a recent Easter School which came at a key moment in the writing of this book, and to staff colleagues John Wigfield, the Revd Linda Boon, Rebecca Watson and Alison Kilburn. I also need to thank students Eve Ridgeway, John Fisher, Chris Herbert and Mark Poole, who showed courage and enterprise in travelling to Tanzania for placements at Bunda Bible College and brought back enthusiasm and energy for its link with St Hild College. I am grateful to the St Hild College council for granting me sabbatical leave in the autumn of 2017 when the interviews in Mara and a large part of the writing took place.

A special word of thanks is due to Bishop Stephen Platten and to my wife Sally, who both read through an almost complete draft of the book and gave some very helpful and constructive feedback.

Without the commissioning of the book by David Shervington and the editorial board at SCM Press it would not have seen the light of day. I am grateful to him and to them.

In February 2018 I left St Hild College and the Tanzania–Leeds Link to start working for the Anglican Communion as its director for Theological Education, based in London. The arena I now work in is global, diverse and complex and not a little daunting. I am hugely grateful for the formation I have received for this role from all of the above people, who have shown what the Anglican Communion can be at its best. Pride of place must go to Bishop Hilkiah Omindo, whose unstinting commitment to his diocese over 20 years of ministry, combined with wonderful humour and humility, released and encouraged its people to make disciples of friends and neighbours and allowed the church to grow and grow. This book is dedicated to him.

Introduction

Many in the churches today want to see growth. But what is genuine church growth? Is it all about the numerical growth of congregations, or are there other dimensions? If so, what are they and how can they be encouraged as a whole? This book addresses these questions in a systematic and reflective way, building on my SCM *Studyguide Christian Mission*, which presented a survey of the roots and history of Christian mission. That book brought the survey into our own time in an exploratory and open-ended way. This book takes it forward in a more focused way, bringing one of the major concerns of contemporary missiology, church growth, to the centre of attention and exploring its meaning and application for our own time. It does this through a case study of some very significant church growth in Tanzania. Then, with commentary from Mwita Akiri, a Tanzanian bishop and academic theologian, it reflects on the wider meaning and importance of what is uncovered there, moving from that context in the global South to the global North and to contemporary Britain and, in particular, to the challenging situation of a fairly typical medium-sized church in a provincial town.

In looking at church growth the book takes its cue from some words of Rowan Williams when he was Archbishop of Canterbury. Speaking to the General Synod of the Church of England in 2010 he set a task that created its agenda for 'reform and renewal' in the years since then. He described how for the church's leadership three main themes

have emerged with absolute clarity. We are called (i) To take forward the spiritual and numerical growth of the Church of England – including the growth of its capacity to serve the whole community of this country; (ii) To re-shape or reimagine the Church's ministry for the century coming, so as to make sure that there is a growing and sustainable Christian witness in every local community; and (iii) To focus our resources where there is both greatest need and greatest opportunity. (Church of England, GS 995)

This statement brings the need for church growth to the centre of Christian mission, not only for the Church of England but for many other denominations in the global North that face similar challenges. Very importantly, it presents a threefold view of church growth, including not just the most obvious dimension of numerical growth – the numbers of those attending church services or signing up as members – but of 'spiritual growth' and of a growth in 'witness in every local community'. It therefore points to the way that church growth is a multi-dimensional phenomenon, reflecting the breadth of ways a church interacts with its surrounding community. Williams then calls for the ministry and the resources of the Church of England to be reconfigured to serve this kind of growth. Others have followed this lead, including the current Archbishop of Canterbury Justin Welby and the missiologist Bob Jackson, who in a number of influential publications has described the importance of seeing growth in these three dimensions (for example, *What Makes Churches Grow?*, pp. 3–4). The pages that follow here explore the multi-dimensional nature of the growth that Williams was calling for, uncovering not just three but six dimensions, which is one of the key findings of this book, and exploring the stages of growth within each. This is for the purpose of understanding and mapping the *ecology* of church growth, meaning the interconnectedness of the church and its growth with its environment, so that the task Williams sets the church may be taken forward in an ever more informed and effective way.

At the heart of the book is a case study based on a series of interviews conducted in the Mara region of Tanzania. Why turn to Mara? The answer is that the Anglican churches in this north-western corner of the country (along with some other denominations) have seen substantial growth over the last 30 years. From a very low base line of a dozen parishes in 1985 the original Mara diocese grew to 150 parishes by 2010, at which point it was divided into three dioceses: Mara, Rorya and Tarime. The two daughter dioceses of Tarime and Rorya have themselves experienced growth in their own right. At the time of writing, Tarime has 4,950 members in 50 congregations, up from 1,100 members and 27 congregations when the diocese was inaugurated in 2010. It is a story of exponential growth, remarkable for Africa as well as for the world church generally, and a story which includes primary evangelism, discipleship, community development in health, education and farming, and much else. It therefore provides a rich and exemplary case study of the phenomenon of church growth, one that offers a different and fresh perspective from current views in the global North.

As the link officer for the diocesan companionship link between Leeds Diocese (previously Wakefield Diocese) in the Church of England and these dioceses of Mara, Rorya and Tarime in Mara region, over the course of eight visits in seven years I have come to know them well and have been inspired by what is happening within them. I have got to know their extensive work in their local communities through primary and secondary education, water projects, agricultural centres, health projects, a safe house and theological colleges. I have been able to interview a cross-section of people at the heart of this church growth, both lay and ordained. The interviews, as will be seen, convey a rich and informative profile. Their insights into the 'why' and 'how' of church growth provide primary source material for a practical missiology and, especially, for reflection on how this 'Mara growth' might be transferred into other contexts such as the one we face in contemporary Britain.

It may be wondered if differences in culture and context would rule out the possibility of such transference. The first section of the book introduces Tanzania in general and Mara region in particular and reveals a number of these differences, some very great. Tanzania is, literally, a world away from Britain. Apart from obvious differences of climate, language, history, culture and economy there are differences of religious outlook and especially of a general receptivity to Christian mission. Over the last 50 years Tanzania has demonstrated remarkable openness to what the churches have to offer, especially to primary evangelism, with church growth taking place in Anglican, Lutheran, Roman Catholic, Methodist, Presbyterian and other mainline traditions as well as within a whole host of Pentecostal and other independent churches. This comes into obvious contrast with the situation of churches in the North and especially in Britain, where many are often resistant to evangelism, and mission must take place in other ways.

Nevertheless, there is significant common ground between the two contexts and of the situation of the church within them. Apart from the people of both places sharing a common humanity under God, with all the challenges and joys of living, growing, loving, suffering and dying on this fertile planet, the Christ whom Christians follow is the same 'yesterday, today and for ever', with the discipleship he offers reflecting this. Furthermore, as Andrew Walls has argued in his widely acclaimed surveys of Christian history and the ebb and flow of mission within it, there is a core to Christian life that runs through every age of Christian history, based on shared 'worship of the God of Israel', of belief in 'the ultimate significance of Jesus of Nazareth', 'that God is active where believers are', 'that believers constitute a people of God transcending time and space' and that there are 'a small body of institutions which have continued from century to century. The most obvious of these have been the reading of a common body of scriptures and the special use of bread and wine and water' (Walls 1996, pp. 23–4). All this gives good grounds for exploring whether the key principles of an approach to church growth in one context can be transferred to another.

4

The pages that follow seek to identify the constituent elements and principles of the Mara approach to such growth, making a special point of finding examples of each of these in the global North and especially in Britain. This increases the likelihood of being able to transfer the approach as a whole; this is explored in the final chapter in a case study of a fairly typical medium-sized British church.

It is important to add that the interviews unsettled my own assumptions, and have taken the reflections in these pages in an unexpected direction. While they provided a rich portrait of a church growing in different directions they revealed within this one especially important element. As I collated what I had been told it became clear that the clergy and lay people were especially enthused about evangelism: the deliberate calling of others to faith. They had plenty to say about church growth but this had not been the primary motivation of what they were doing. Their preoccupation was the work of sharing the gospel of salvation with others, in word and deed, and this needed to be reflected in these pages.

I did not at first find this a very welcome insight. I had long been wary of the word 'evangelism'. In my mind it was too closely connected with 'Bible bashing', the forceful and unthinking imposition of Christian dogmas on non-believers. My educational background was in a tradition of dialogue, debate and the critical weighing up of the case for Christian belief. Emotion and experience played a part but only after reason had shown that it was not unreasonable to do so. The word 'evangelism' evoked images of mass rallies with emotional coercion at play in the rhetoric of usually male and usually American speakers. I found the archetypal evangelistic rally ethically dubious and unattractive. I was very committed to the word 'mission', seeing it as broad and inclusive, expressing the diverse range of ways the church interacts with society and participates in the work of God. But 'evangelism' was the slightly embarrassing country cousin who needed to be kept in the back room while sophisticated cosmopolitan guests were welcomed in the front room. So to be led back to the importance of evangelism by my Tanzanian friends was not what I had been expecting. Yet led I was, over the period of researching and writing this book, and to a point where I am keen to affirm its importance.

As will become clear through the chapters that follow, I now believe that evangelism has a leading role in any attempt to bring growth to the church. But my encounter with Mara's evangelism has shown that it should not be conceived in the caricatured way described above. As I discovered, there is a much more engaging way to conceive it when it is seen within a wider network of community relationships.

This book, then, is first an account of that journey of exploration, beginning with the reports of my Tanzanian friends and colleagues who opened up for me the rich and multi-dimensional phenomenon of church growth in Mara. It includes commentary from Mwita Akiri, the Bishop of Tarime, and with his help seeks to distil the key elements of that church growth in a clear and systematic way, identifying the leading role of evangelism within the mix and highlighting its distinctive and sometimes unexpected features. Then, based on the conviction that the renewal of the church comes not from the established and wealthy centres of Christendom but from its margins, where hard-pressed Christians rediscover the simple and profound message of the gospel, the book asks the critical question of whether and how this whole approach to church growth could be embraced and expressed within the mission of the churches of the global North, and in particular in Britain. It comes not only from the most economically marginal continent in the world but within that from one of the most marginal regions of Tanzania itself. It is, I believe, a wonderful and precious gift, which reveals the secret of church growth for others. This book is an attempt to share that gift with those who are eager for such growth in other parts of the world.

I

A Tanzanian Journey

At the Margins and at the Centre

Tanzania sits just below the equator in East Africa, with the Indian Ocean to its east and the vast expanse of Lake Victoria and Lake Tanganyika to the west. Why turn to such a far-off country when exploring church growth in the global North? Tanzania is, after all, at the margins of the modern world, away from the economic powerhouses of North America, the Far East, the Indian subcontinent and Europe. Maps of global flight paths show a dense conglomeration in the northern hemisphere, especially over North America and Europe, and a striking sparsity over sub-Saharan Africa. Maps of global internet traffic paint a similar picture, with heavy traffic across the northern hemisphere and a fraction of that traffic in the southern. Maps of GDP density show many parts of the northern hemisphere with a high density, often coloured red or a deep crimson for the highest of all (Japan, parts of China, parts of Europe and the eastern half and west coast of North America), with most of Africa in the lower, paler categories. Tanzania is clearly and obviously in these lower categories.

Similarly in terms of the human development index – a comparative measure of life expectancy, literacy, education and standards of living that measures well-being, especially in child welfare (as developed by Pakistani economist Mahbub ul Haq and Indian economist Amartya Sen) – Tanzania is in the bottom quartile. This is illustrated in the fact that in a population of around 58 million just under half do not have access to basic clean water supplies and only a quarter have access to adequate sanitation. It is estimated that in the rural areas women and children spend over two hours a day collecting water, and up to seven hours in remote areas, and that each year 20,000 children die of diarrhoeal diseases before the age of five. Infant mortality in general is between 70 and 80 per 1,000, and approximately one-third of the population live below the poverty line, with an average life expectancy of around 57 years. These are shocking statistics in a world of increasing and extraordinary wealth for many. They reinforce the sense that despite some recent improvements in the economy this is a country being left behind by the global economic juggernaut.

Yet a very different picture can be painted. Tanzania contains one of the oldest known inhabited areas on Earth. Fossil remains of humans and pre-human hominids dating back over two million years have been found in the Olduvai Gorge of the Ngorongoro area. It is a region of rich anthropological history, originally populated by hunter-gatherer communities, probably Cushitic and Khoisan-speaking people, followed about 2,000 years ago by Bantu-speaking people beginning to arrive from western Africa in a series of migrations. Later still, Nilotic pastoralists arrived, and continued to immigrate into the area through to the eighteenth century.

All this means that today there are more than 120 distinct ethnic groups and tribes in Tanzania. None of them are dominant, which means that since independence in the early 1960s Tanzania has been spared the tribal conflicts experienced in other post-independence nations. The peacefulness of the country also comes from its people not only speaking their own tribal languages but widely communicating in Swahili, a Bantu language that acts as a lingua franca in many parts of East Africa, where it developed through the interaction of the people with Arab traders from at least the seventeenth century onwards. Kiswahili is a bond that unites the diverse peoples of Tanzania, whereas in other African countries the people of different tribes can only communicate with one another in English, French or Portuguese (if they can speak

those languages). The founding president of Tanzania, Julius
Nyerere, himself from Mara region, is widely recognized as
laying the foundations of unity in the country with his respectful and fatherly style of leadership. He is often referred to as
'mwalimu' (teacher) and 'baba wa taifa' (father of the nation)
and is remembered with affection and reverence to this day.
Mwita Akiri adds:

Nyerere preached and taught Tanzanians that they are all
brother or sister to one another. In a country of more than
120 ethnic groups each with a distinct culture and customs,
Nyerere successfully built a sense of nationhood enjoyed by
very few African countries. The word he used, which is still
used widely by Tanzanians and by which many address one
another today, is 'ndugu'. It is neither masculine nor femi-
nine, and neither singular nor plural. Therefore, it cannot be
translated as 'brethren', which implies more than one person. 'Ndugu' signifies the fact that whoever you see next to
you is someone with whom you share kinship. Because of
this, Tanzania has been spared from the civil wars that one
hears about in many African countries.

While it is important to acknowledge sources of potential conflict in the divide between Christians and Muslims, especially
along the east coast and on the island of Zanzibar, these have
not resulted in the kind of inter-religious violence found in
neighbouring countries. Tanzania's peaceful example of community life may not, then, be quite as marginal to the needs of
the modern world as first impressions may suggest.

Tanzania's natural environment is hugely impressive and of
great importance to the continent and the world as a whole.
Its lakes provide rich resources of fish; in the Indian Ocean
are recently discovered natural gas fields. It is a vast country
of 365,000 square miles (compared to the UK's 94,000 square
miles). It is a physically stunning environment, with the highest mountain in Africa, Kilimanjaro, at 5,895 metres (19,341
feet), and the second largest freshwater lake in the world, Lake
Victoria, shared with Uganda and Kenya and roughly the size

of Wales. There are large areas of dry savannah and semi-desert in the north, and rich forests in the south. Many areas are fertile and, provided it rains, produce abundant crops to feed Tanzania's own population and export to other nations.

Moreover, Tanzania has one of the largest concentrations of wild animals in the world, mainly found in the northern areas between Mount Kilimanjaro in the east and the Mara River in the west, mostly in protected parks and reserves which together form one of the largest wildlife havens in Africa. The worth and importance of these reserves should not be under-estimated in a world that is increasingly losing its wild areas and diversity of animal species. A visitor to these areas can gain a powerful experience of the richness and wonder of nature not found in urban and semi-urban environments. In terms of providing an opportunity to come to know humanity's place in the natural order of things, Tanzania must be recognized as being of central importance to the human race.

The people of Tanzania have much to teach other societies about self-sufficiency. A majority of Tanzanian households practise subsistence farming, ploughing and cultivating their shambas (fields) where they grow staple crops such as maize, sorghum, millet, rice, wheat, beans, cassava, potatoes and bananas (depending on the levels of rainfall). They will also produce their own mud bricks, baking and hardening them in purpose-built kilns, to construct their homes. They will conserve and recycle most household items. They spend a morning each week – if a business, a day each month – cleaning up the areas surrounding where they live and work (under direction from the government). All this shows a very high degree of sustainability as well as self-sufficiency from which the consumer societies of the developed world have much to learn. Efforts are also under way to counteract widespread deforestation around the growing urban areas, and to reduce the pollution of Lake Victoria and other areas of high population density. Once again, Tanzania demonstrates a cluster of virtues that many people in other parts of the world can learn from. It is far from being a marginal place.

The recently elected government of Tanzania is committed to fighting corruption and mismanagement. President John Magufuli, elected in October 2015 and known to be a results-driven, 'no-nonsense' figure, has vowed to stamp out corruption in public office, government departments and state corporations. One of his recent campaigns has been to rein in some of the multi-national mining corporations, such as Barrick Gold, who were found to have been exporting large quantities of ore without declaring all types of minerals found in the ore other than gold ore and therefore not paying the required taxes. Magufuli has held his nerve and provided a powerful example for other governments to follow. He is, though, acquiring a reputation as an autocrat.

The Tanzanian national flag in some ways embodies the reasons why this young nation has much to offer the wider world. The green corner of the flag symbolizes the produce of the land, the crops grown by its self-sufficient and enterprising people. They in turn are represented by a central black strip reaching across from corner to corner. The wealth of the Indian Ocean and inland lakes is represented by a blue corner of the flag, and Tanzania's extensive geological wealth is symbolized by two gold strips that divide the green and the blue.

But there is another set of reasons for seeing Tanzania not on the margins but at the centre of the world, and these are connected with the concerns of this book: missiology. They arise from the way the Tanzanian church is part of a wider and very dramatic movement of church growth across sub-Saharan Africa in the twentieth and twenty-first centuries. William L. Sachs describes this from an Anglican perspective but what he writes applies to other denominations as well:

The most striking instance of the Church's growth and its diversification occurred in sub-Saharan Africa. There, over the course of the twentieth century, the Church's following increased nearly one hundredfold, from barely half a million to almost fifty million people ... By the early twenty-first century, Anglicanism's distribution, as much as its numerical

growth, had changed its character. In 1900 over 80 per cent
of adherents lived in Britain; by 2005 only one-third were
found there while over half were African. (Sachs 2018,
pp. 1–2)

Furthermore, within the community of African Anglican
churches the Anglican Church of Tanzania (ACT) deserves
special mention because of the unique way it has grown out
of two distinct ecclesial movements, the Evangelical and the
Anglo-Catholic traditions; it was the product of the work of
two missionary societies in the mid-nineteenth century, namely
the Universities' Mission to Central Africa (UMCA) and the
Church Missionary Society (CMS). The former was founded
in the wake of David Livingstone's call to bring Christianity
to Africa and from a base on the island of Zanzibar planted
mission stations and dioceses on the mainland from the 1860s
onwards. CMS, based in the Church of England and founded
in 1799, brought Evangelical Anglicanism to central Tanzania
especially from the 1870s onwards and to Mara region through
African catechists who crossed the border from Kenya in the
1930s. Of ACT's 28 dioceses, eight are Anglo-Catholic and 20
are Evangelical in tradition. Since seceding from the Province
of East Africa in 1970, it has developed a structure of provincial government that holds these traditions together under an
elected archbishop, one prayer book, a national constitution,
a house of bishops, a provincial synod of bishops, clergy and
laity, and a national standing committee, served by a secre-
tariat in the nation's capital of Dodoma. This holding structure
is complemented by each diocese being semi-autonomous. The
archbishop has only advisory status within the dioceses, unless
there is a vacancy and an election must be organized. This
level of diocesan autonomy, with each diocese able to fully
inhabit whichever tradition it comes from, is one of the reasons
why the province has successfully held together these different
church traditions.

Behind this structural unity, furthermore, is agreement over
a common ground of doctrine and practice. It is worth quoting

a full summary of this from Tanzanian theologians Phanuel L. Mung'ong'o and Moses Matonya's recent profile of ACT in the *Wiley-Blackwell Companion to the Anglican Communion*. This summary shows the extent of the agreement:

> The centre of the ACT's teaching is the life, ministry, death, and resurrection of Jesus Christ. The following statements are part of the teaching.
> – Jesus Christ is fully human and fully God.
> – He died and was raised from the dead by God the Father.
> – Jesus is the saviour who provides the way of eternal life for those who believe.
> – The Old and New Testaments of the Bible were written by people 'inspired by the Holy Spirit'. The Apocrypha are additional books that are used in Christian teaching, but not for the formation of doctrine.
> – The two great and necessary sacraments are Holy Baptism and Holy Eucharist.
> – Other sacramental rites include confirmation, ordination, marriage, reconciliation of a penitent, and unction.
> – Belief in heaven, hell, resurrection of the dead, and Jesus' return in glory to judge the world.
> The threefold sources of authority typical of Anglicanism (scripture, tradition, and reason, which critique each other in a dynamic way, as proposed by Richard Hooker in the sixteenth century) determine ACT's doctrine. Scripture is primary with tradition and reason augmenting the threefold doctrine, and things stated plainly in scripture are accepted as true. Issues that are ambiguous are determined by tradition, which is checked by reason. (Mung'ong'o and Matonya 2013, pp. 205–6)

This statement shows how ACT builds its unity in diversity on a traditional and unexceptional version of Anglicanism found in many parts of the world with roots going back to the sixteenth century and beyond that to the creeds of the early church. It demonstrates how in theological and ecclesiological terms it is far from being a marginal church but embodies a central and typical form of Anglicanism, so offering a significant degree of common ground on the basis of which its distinctive gifts and charisms can be appreciated all the more clearly.

But what of the differences in culture between rural Africans and urban Europeans or Americans? Do these not rule out transferability of models of mission and growth? In their overview of ACT, Mung'ong'o and Matonya clearly acknowledge how many Tanzanian Anglicans come from a background of traditional cultures and religions, either directly or through being born to parents from the same. They comment that 'ACT is friendly to followers of traditional religions but is strongly opposed to any syncretism among Anglicans,' going on to elaborate this:

> Christians live within clans and families who still believe in traditional religions and other religions such as Islam, Sikhism, and Hinduism, and do things together at family, community, and national levels. They are together in social and community activities, such as weddings, funerals and businesses. However, Christians are not supposed to take part in other religious matters. Some Anglicans regard traditional religions as pagan, superstitious, and even devilish, and tend to ignore and dismiss any element of practice in the Church which seems to relate to traditional religion and culture. However, some turn to traditional religion secretly in times of difficulty. (Mung'ong'o and Matonya 2013, p. 208)

Here is a clear line being drawn between the two. It shows that the differences are not allowed to compromise the Christian faith and practice of the church, which in turn means that it can still offer an authentic expression of Christianity to the wider world. However, it is not a narrow-minded rejection of everything connected with traditional religion and culture. The authors acknowledge that there is dialogue and some fruitful influence across the line:

Inculturation and indigenisation of the gospel compels the
Anglican Church to incorporate some cultural practices into
Christianity. Traditional musical instruments and traditional
ways of singing are allowed in the Church. Traditional styles
of blessing farms and praying for the livestock and proper-
ties of individual Christians in their respective places and
home are adapted in the name of Christ. (Mung'ong'o and
Matonya 2013, p. 208)

ACT, then, embodies a genuinely Christian and Anglican form
of the faith which creates common ground with other Anglican
churches around the world. On the basis of this common
ground these other churches can then learn from what is distinctive and creative in the life of ACT. This applies as much to
mission and growth as to other aspects of its life. This is why
the following chapters turn their attention to this church and
its experience.

But why look specifically at the church in Mara region? The
answer is not just because it provides an example of the church
growth I have direct experience of. It is also because of the
remarkable statistics concerning church growth. Some more
detail can now be given about this growth. The Diocese of Mara
was created in 1985, carved out of the northern section of the
Diocese of Victoria Nyanza, which surrounded Lake Victoria.
At this point there were just 12 'parishes' (established congregations with their own pastor and buildings), and no diocesan
infrastructure. Under the first bishop the number of parishes
more than doubled, growing to 30. The second bishop, Hilkiah
Omindo Deya, was consecrated in 1994 and during the first 13
years of his leadership there was exponential growth, with 107
parishes established by 2007. It is a story, as mentioned earlier,
that includes not just primary evangelism and discipleship but
community development in health, education, water provision
and farming, and much else. Multiplication continued apace,
so that by 2010 there were 143 parishes. At this point Bishop
Hilkiah argued that there were now too many parishes for
him to know all his clergy and congregations and the diocese

should be split. His diocesan synod accepted the argument and in 2010 the Diocese of Rorya, with 44 parishes, was carved out of the north-west corner of Mara, and the Diocese of Tarime, with 29 parishes, out of north-east corner, leaving Mara Diocese in the south with 70 parishes. Since then growth has continued though not at quite the same rate. Small congregations are started in new villages and when these bodies become sufficiently well established they become fully fledged parishes. The dynamics of this process are the subject of the chapters that follow. Clearly the pace and reach of the growth across the region in this period has been hugely impressive and it obviously justifies close attention. It is also a case study I am in a position to describe and reflect on, with help from Mwita Akiri. (For a fuller account of church life and growth in Mara region, see Jones 2013)

But first, to place all this growth in its proper setting, I give an account of the realities of church life at local level, from my personal perspective.

On the Ground

The road from the town descends through some rocky hills on to the plain. Fresh green vegetation, that has sprung up after first rains, soon disappears behind us. The land here is bone dry, the earth parched and cracked. Gusts of wind whip up sand into small whirlwinds. Bedraggled herds of cattle with protruding ribs are cajoled by their young herdsmen. It is not clear where they are going as there is no green grass in sight and the herdsmen are not allowed to move their cattle out of the immediate area. Once we are in the village, an extended series of homesteads spread over a wide area, shapes can be seen lying on the ground in the distance. As we draw near the dreadful reality of the situation becomes clear: these are the bodies of dead cattle, lying in the sun and beginning to decompose. Further on the number of bodies multiplies, some now mauled by local dogs. There are too many for the villagers to bury. The stench of death hangs around the homesteads. My companion, from the local diocese, says that he has never seen this before in this region. The drought that began three years ago is now taking its toll. If it continues, how will the people themselves survive?

The scene is very depressing. It is my third visit to this village; I already knew that it was a drought-prone area and that help was needed from outside. Over the previous couple of years I had encouraged fundraising at home for the drilling of a borehole, so that the villagers would not need to walk 5km to the shores of Lake Victoria for water. The fundraising had gone well, with a number of people giving sacrificially. Thousands of pounds was sent and a drilling company paid to do a survey and sink the borehole. The first attempt, down to 122 metres, failed to yield water. So a second attempt was made, a little further away, down to a similar depth. The devastating news was that this had also failed to yield enough water, and now the drought was taking hold with a vengeance.

Why could not something more be done? Why would the Tanzanian government not come and save the cattle, or at least bury them? Why did the people have to lose the animals in which their livelihoods were invested? Why did those who have so little have to lose even the little they have? Questions and frustration mounted up.

But then we arrive at the small mud-brick, tin-roof church. As we get out of the car we can hear singing and when we go inside the church we find a crowd of people caught up in dance and song, led by a choir of young people smartly dressed in matching brightly coloured batik material and filling the place with life and movement. It is enthralling and humbling. Then, during the service, it becomes clear that some of the older people are caught up in the intercessions, adding their own affirmations, raising their hands, being transported by the worship. Even if desperation brings them to church they are not dwelling on their misfortunes but lifting their minds and hearts to something greater than the hard land they live on. They are caught up in a grace and joy that somehow transforms this little church into a kind of gateway to something greater. The contrast with what is outside is stark. It stops my dejection and frustration in its tracks. It does not remove the need for drought relief but places the whole situation within a bigger and more hopeful context. This bears fruit after the service when the congregation has a community meeting to discuss the drought and decide on what should be done next. Through the discussion a consensus emerges on the need to work with the local government in seeking resources to find a different solution. It is clear that both the worship and the meeting have helped to energize and inspire the people to work together to try to overcome the effects of the drought.

This is not an isolated example. Over the seven years I visited Mara I found a number of other churches where there was a similar combination of acute need and irrepressible Christian life. On top of this were the simple facts of church growth in this region. Over 25 years Mara Diocese had grown by over a hundredfold. At its creation in 1985, as already mentioned, the diocese had a dozen parishes plus a large section of the Serengeti national park (including one million wildebeest on their annual migration!). Following the division of the diocese into three in 2010, growth continued, with four or five new parishes established most years. And this church growth has not just been about congregational enlargement: it has gone hand in hand with a range of development projects at parish and diocesan level, from weekday children's nurseries to digging wells for drinking water to pastoral and medical support for victims of HIV/AIDS. Church schools have been started and extended, agricultural development work has taken place and theological education extended.

If such growth was possible in Tanzania then maybe it could happen in Britain? It has certainly happened here in the past, through the Evangelical revival of the eighteenth century, the Catholic revival of the nineteenth century and the growth of social action in the twentieth. Why not a fresh revival in our own century? Given the lack of overall progress in renewing and growing churches in Britain in the last decade, Tanzania could provide an example that offers clues to a promising way forward. To find out if this might be the case I needed to explore the causes and development of this flourishing expression of church life.

I decided I would turn to church growth in Mara and explore its dynamics. I would begin with the personal reasons why people had become Christians and joined their local church, because ultimately church growth is about actual people deciding to commit to Christ and become his disciples. Beginning at the local level, then, with the experience of new Christians, the question would be this: what was drawing these people into an active Christian faith? Only after answering this would I then explore the steps the church leadership had taken to enable this to happen and look at how the new Christians were being supported by clergy and lay ministers. Finally, Mwita Akiri, as one of the bishops of the region, would add his thoughts on the causes and dynamics of this growth at different points in the narrative, so helping to identify the key themes of this remarkable story.

Voices of New Christians

My listening began at a diocesan theological college, a small collection of breezeblock buildings in a flat and dusty plot of ground some distance from the nearest town. The men shared tiny rooms with bunk beds and communal washing facilities. The women had their own hostel building which was again small for the numbers in it. Many had left wives, husbands and small children at home in order to come and train for ministry. It did not seem a very promising environment in which to equip and inspire them to become catechists, evangelists and ordained pastors. But appearances can be deceptive. I quickly saw that this was a group of people who were committed to and energized by their studies and practical preparation for serving God. Many were fairly new to the Christian faith and all were in touch with other new Christians in their home churches in the villages of the diocese. For these reasons they were a good group to work with to find out about church growth in this region. My first question, then, was a simple one: what drew these people to becoming Christians?

One ordinand from the drought-prone Serengeti district was very clear: it was the message about the kingdom of God. In the face of fear of all kinds, of hunger, illness, conflict, witchcraft and death, it gives people security, it makes them feel safe and secure. This brief but suggestive answer immediately showed that one important dimension of church growth had been effective communication of a definite gospel message: these new Christians had been taught, had heard and owned for themselves Christ's teaching of the coming of the kingdom of God, a message that in the face of many kinds of hardship gave them hope and assurance.

Another ordinand reported that it was the mutual support of his Anglican congregation that had attracted new members, especially the way members help each other and care for those in need. It was a case of actions speaking louder than words: 'The members of the church are well respected in the community.' This shows a second dimension of the growth – the quality of community life within the church. There had been a genuine and practical mutuality in the way its members related to each other.

For another it had been the gospel message about Jesus, that he is the saviour and forgives their sins: 'When you come and give your life to him you can live a life free of worldly burdens – conflict, adultery, witchcraft, gossip.' This suggests that entering into meaningful discipleship, living a transformed life as a follower of Jesus, had been a key to faith and growth.

Another factor mentioned by others was the liveliness of the worship in their churches, where a choir knowing the words of the worship songs by heart would sing and dance together, expressively moving in time with each other, backed by a loud PA system, filling the church and surrounding neighbourhood with gospel music. This had brought many to the church, especially the young, who love to play an active part in worship.

Akiri later explained the cultural background to this, referring to the tribal identity of many of these people as Kuria, a pastoralist-agriculturalist group found in north-western Tanzania and particularly his Diocese of Tarime and in parts of the Diocese of Mara, especially the Serengeti district: 'Kuria society is a partying society – the people like to enjoy themselves. Parties create an opportunity for socializing and creating bonds among those involved whether in church or in the community. Youth choirs are very attractive to other young people.'

This could be described as a sacramental dimension to church life, in which the gospel message is communicated not only in words but also in active experience, through music and dance, a physical and dynamic expression that makes real the faith, hope and love of Christ for those people. A sacrament is defined as 'an outward and visible sign of an inward and spiritual grace' (from the Catechism of The Book of Common Prayer) and here, it seems, is a good example of this. It also links with a first-millennium understanding of sacraments as including a wide range of things and experiences (see p. 80) that were 'hinting symbols or types in which the old order is seen as an anticipation of the new: a hidden, partially comprehended sense that is only fully understood in retrospect' (David Brown in Rowell and Hall 2004, p. 24). Furthermore, the broadcasting of music to the local neighbourhood shows that the sign is not just for the congregation but for the surrounding community as well.

Other ordinands mentioned the diocesan development projects. One of them, from Tarime, described how the diocesan farm development centre had brought local farmers to its training courses and this had made them aware of the existence of the Anglican church. They had been impressed with its involvement in the community; some subsequently wanted to join it. Other projects that had made an impact were the church's support of families with HIV and AIDS, especially a goat project that had lent out goats to such families so that they could have the nutritious milk from the goats and keep the offspring. The digging of community wells in the Diocese of Mara and the harvesting of rainwater in the Diocese of Tarime for safe drinking water had also made an impact. All this can be described as the servant dimension of church growth, where the church reaches out to serve the most pressing needs of the local community. It is a service that is rendered for its own sake and not with any ulterior motive but it nevertheless contributes to the standing and the growth of the church community.

Another ordinand from Mara Diocese reported that the message that Jesus is able to heal their sickness and answer their problems has touched many people, especially when they had seen church people visit and care for certain people in the community who had been abandoned by their families. These church people had gone into homes and prayed with those who lived there and shared the word of God, encouraging people that 'even though they had been abandoned by their own families they were still part of God's family'. This included visiting and caring for widows and orphans. When others had seen this they said that these Christians are 'the true church'. This again shows the servant dimension of church growth as well as the importance of supportive relationships within the congregation.

Akiri comments:

Our people have a big sense of sin and salvation. To be saved is to be saved from sin. It is not so much about feeling guilty and fearing going to the fires of hell. Very little preaching now dwells on this. It is more about God's love and following Christ out of darkness to lead a full life. The imagery of coming out of darkness and into the light is very important to people. There is not much concern with the second coming of Jesus Christ, though people are aware that the world will end at some point. It is about getting out of sin and into salvation. They recognize a clear distinction between the two states. Having said this, there is a great need for good teaching about faith, for this converts people on the inside. The message that we are made in God's image and he loves us is important to the people.

All this also highlights the effectiveness of the communication in his churches. The people have heard and appropriated for themselves the gospel message: they have a clear sense of having moved from one domain to another, in the here and now. It also shows how they have embraced discipleship and that it is a reality in their lives. While more teaching is needed, and more printed resources in Swahili are needed to support this, a message of reconciliation in the here and now has been communicated to many people and they have responded with a genuine and often enthusiastic discipleship.

Akiri draws a revealing distinction with Pentecostalism:

[Our people] are less concerned in coming to church for healing, including exorcism. There is a ministry of healing within services, sometimes at the start or at the end, but this is not the main reason people are there, unlike within Pentecostal worship. At the big open-air meetings we run there may be some people who come forward for deliverance and the number varies from place to place. The title that best sums up our people's view of Jesus is 'Saviour' – this captures what appeals to them about him. The increasingly popular refrain 'Bwana Yesu asifiwe' (Praise Jesus the Lord) reflects this.

Anyone who has visited Mara region will know that this phrase is not just said but is shouted with passion and excitement at every possible opportunity. The effective communication in Mara therefore includes an interactive element, in which the people internalize what they have learnt from preaching and repeat a rousing refrain to reinforce it.

This interactive element and enthusiasm of sharing one's faith is facilitated by two things. First is the fact that unlike the developed world where many own cars and the public transport system is elaborate, and electronic communication minimizes human interaction, the level of human interaction in Tanzania and other developing countries is intense. This remains the case despite the arrival of mobile phones on the scene from around the year 2000. The majority of people in rural areas and in cities and towns travel on foot. Even when they use public transport, it is not uncommon for it to hardly get them anywhere near their homes. It is therefore easy for people to meet one another in the open space. Communal events such as weddings and funerals also provide opportunity for interaction, not only for pastors and lay ministers to preach but for people to share the word of God as people walk back home after the event.

This section began by asking the question of what was drawing people into an active Christian faith. The first set of answers from students at the theological college, together with Akiri's commentary, have highlighted five elements in what churches are offering: effective communication of the gospel, mutual support in congregational life, powerful 'sacramental' expression of the faith, service of the wider community and meaningful discipleship. There will have been other factors that helped create a conducive environment for growth, such as a widespread cultural openness to Christian belief, as mentioned in the Introduction, and effective church leadership that has facilitated these elements, but these five factors have been identified by the students and so these are the ones to highlight.

But this is quite a generalized answer to the question. To discover more detail and texture, the views of some experienced church leaders who have spent several years engaging with these issues are needed.

The Pastor

In Tarime Diocese a parish priest, usually called a pastor, spoke of his experience of church growth. A tall and bright-eyed young man, who greeted me with the lovely Swahili phrase 'karibu' (you are welcome), he was enthusiastic about his ministry in his remote parish of subsistence farmers. He reaffirmed what the ordinands had said about the importance of community service by the diocese:

Often [the people we visit] have heard about the Anglican church and its farm development work. They may have come to the farm development centre for training. This makes the Christian faith more attractive.

He then spoke at some length and in rich detail about how the gospel message is communicated. He described a one-to-one element when bringing people to faith, a personal evangelism that he did on a weekly basis, usually on a Thursday:

The plan is to have house-to-house evangelism, going in pairs. We start with visiting the homes of the congregation and then move on to non-believers. When welcomed into a home I first introduce myself as a pastor from the Anglican church and that we have come to have a discussion about God, Jesus and the Bible. If they say this is OK we might sing a worship song, then sit and pray and then I will tell them about how God has created the world and that Christians believe in this great God rather than the small gods of pagans. I will tell them the message of John 1, that the Word of God was there from the beginning and that nothing has happened without God: so God is the God of all, he is the first and the last, everything is in his hands. I talk about the birth of Jesus, that God has come among us, and of the miracles of Jesus and the difference he makes to our lives.

This is a revealing testimony. It shows that the communication between evangelists and hosts is predicated on the friendliness and vulnerability of the evangelists: they have come into the home of those they are talking to and depend on the welcome and hospitality of that home. The power dynamics of the classroom, where the teacher has power over the students to pass or fail their work, is absent. Instead they come offering a gift in friendship, a gift that can be accepted or refused. Furthermore, they offer their teaching only if there is assent from their host: the power lies with the student, not the teacher, as it were. The principle here is not about evangelistic communication having to take place in a home, for in some contexts this is not possible, but about the communicator being like a guest to a host wherever they happen to be meeting.

It is important to note that the singing of a worship song and the saying of a prayer explicitly brings a third party into the room, which is God's presence. This means that the communication taking place is not just the relaying of information from one party to the other. Something more is being encouraged, an engagement with the one who surrounds and dwells within them all. The teaching, then, is not only going to point to the gospel of God, it is somehow going to bring it into effect. The 'sacramental' element found in the worship of the choir, then, can also be found in the intimacy of this home teaching.

The testimony shows how the content of the teaching mediates between two different realities: the cultural world of the hosts, influenced by traditional pagan religion, and Christian faith rooted in the Bible of both Old and New Testaments. The teaching is a sensitive yet challenging presentation of the latter to the former. What is offered is different and definite, not a simple accommodation of what is there already. This is possible because of the vulnerability of the teachers: they are not imposing what they bring but simply laying it on the table.

The fundamental respect of the relationship between hosts and teachers is again emphasized:

I always give them the opportunity to choose whether to become a Christian. I offer to come back to continue the conversation. They choose a day which will suit them. If they say they are not sure I will leave them with a Bible verse to read and discuss later. One I often use is Psalm 95.1: 'O come let us sing to the Lord; let us make a joyful noise to the rock of our salvation.' I will write it on a piece of paper so that they can meditate on it. If they are old and do not read I will give it to a younger member of the family to read out to them.

This shows the door being opened to active discipleship for the hosts. They can freely choose whether to set out on the path of following Christ, and some words of scripture are given to encourage them along this path. But note that there is no implied threat of hellfire and damnation. The gift that is being offered is something joyful and life-giving. However, there is an edge to this gift relevant to a context in which FGM is still practised:

I will also challenge them about FGM. I will say that in the Bible we are told that all that God created is good – so why harm it. I will challenge them to change their life.

The outcome of this encounter can lay a strong foundation for future discipleship:

If and when they become a Christian they feel they are freed from fear of evil spirits and that demons and devils have been chased away and it is no longer necessary to wear charms. Their protection is now from God.

This liberating message is not restricted to home visiting, how-ever. Open-air preaching also takes place:

Sometimes the house-to-house visiting will be supplemented with an open-air meeting. Members of the choir will sing and dance gospel songs near the village centre, with the PA system (powered by a portable generator). We will have singing and preaching between 3pm and 5pm on a Thursday (after people have finished work). My message is that Jesus is calling us to leave our burdens and come to him, to come from the darkness and into the light, because Jesus is the light of the world. I invite people to come forward so that we can pray with them. Those who have problems with their families or marriages come forward, and sometimes those being persecuted by devils. Then we ask where they are living and whether they would like a visit. If they would, we go and see them. We normally visit two to three homes each week.

Communication, then, is to take place in the public square as well as in the home. The church will confidently present the gospel message to any who will choose to come and listen. It will do this through preaching and through a choir, with lively singing and dancing. As already argued, this brings the reality of God's salvation into bodily expression in music and movement, which for some becomes as important as the verbal communication. At the end of his testimony, however, we see the pastor emphasizing the primacy of one-to-one conversation. What is the outcome of all this evangelism?

Each time we do an open-air meeting and follow up with home visits we find that two or three new people come to church on Sunday morning. So our church is growing: when I arrived in 2014 there were 30 adults and 50 children coming to church. Now in 2017 there are 80 adults and around 100 children. Our church building is becoming too small. We have planted a new church in a neighbouring hamlet, which is nearer to where some of the congregation live. Now they worship there. Meanwhile we need to build a vicarage and then enlarge the church. On Wednesdays we fetch stones and make bricks for the new vicarage. The financial giving of the people is small because they are poor, but when it is harvest time they are generous, giving in kind.

The communication of the gospel in word and sacrament, then, with encouragement and support to become disciples of Christ, leads to modest but steady institutional growth. Attendances increase, regular membership increases, giving (in kind) increases and the material resources of the church are developed. It is important to note, however, that the pastor's primary intention is not to increase the size of the church: our conversation has shown that his passion is to communicate the liberating gospel of Christ to the people of his community, so that they may be freed from all that oppresses them and become joy-filled disciples of Christ. This is his priority.

Akiri adds:

Lay ministers are key. While they are clerically led they are the ones who work at the grass roots and who form a kind of lay movement committed to spreading the faith, they organize themselves, they know how to collect food and to go and sleep in another parish or deanery to evangelize. They are self-funding, receiving no outside support. They are self-motivated, responding to the command of Jesus in Matthew 28 to make disciples of all (though they rarely cross tribal or district boundaries). They are also aware that we are a small diocese and we need to grow. They manage on their own with the bishop only turning up on a Sunday and giving them a lead and encouragement in their work.

In many ways this reflects Church Missionary Society tradition, which founded the Anglican Church in this part of East Africa, with mission being 'self-extending, self-supporting, self-governing'. There has been a historic prominence of lay ministers in evangelism and even discipleship (see, for example, Akiri 1999 and Piroute 1978). The number of expatriate missionaries on the ground was always small in relation to the vast areas that had to be evangelized. Consequently, clergy and lay missionaries had to recruit and rely on African converts and catechists to evangelize their own people in the villages and establish churches under administrative supervision of the foreign missionaries. These local often young converts knew the culture and the environment better and became indispensable in the expansion of Christianity in many parts of Africa.

The results were often impressive. Today lay ministers continue to play a significant role in evangelism and in establishing initial community relationships. Most of these experienced lay ministers go on to train as ordinands and become pastors and a few become bishops. In this way, it is fair to say that almost all pastors, and some bishops, retain a degree of the 'fire' of evangelism burning inside them.

For them and many African Christians and church leaders, faith is not a private commodity [as it is in many traditional non-evangelical churches in Britain]. It is a gift of God to be shared by all who do not have a personal relationship with Jesus Christ and are not his children according to John 1.12.

Fortunately, religious freedom in Tanzania means not only freedom of worship but also the freedom to evangelize, as long as one does not break the law by forcing people to come to faith by abusing other faiths, be it Christianity, Islam, Hindu or even African traditional religion.

All this testifies to the quality of congregational life in growing churches. Those who come to worship come not only to receive but also to give: they have a sense of ownership and responsibility for what takes place and are committed to extending it under their own steam and with their own resources. They are wanting not just to preserve what they have been given, but to propagate and hand it on to others.

The pastor, then, significantly enhances the picture of church growth presented by the ordinands. He demonstrates that doors are opened by the church's work of community service. He shows that the effective communication of the gospel is based on the friendliness and vulnerability of evangelists as they go to the homes of enquirers, and that in certain specific respects their teaching is challenging to their hosts. Communication is not only in words but is expressed in song and dance in the public square, a 'sacramental' expression for all the community. Discipleship is offered as a gift, not a threat, as a way to find liberation from fear and oppression. Akiri underlines the way that the quality of community life within the congregation plays an important part in the self-extension of the church in this region: their sense of ownership and commitment makes them want to bring others into the faith. Church growth, then, is a multi-dimensional phenomenon: the numerical growth of the institution is only one aspect of something broader and richer.

The Director of Evangelism

The pastor is concerned with one or two churches, sometimes a few more. The diocesan director of evangelism, from Mara Diocese, on the other hand, takes a bigger view, looking at a district as a whole and developing an evangelistic strategy. A larger than life figure, able to stand out in a crowd, he introduced himself to me with the words, 'Evangelism is in my blood.' He has been instrumental in starting a host of churches in different parts of his diocese.

He described how his approach begins with a survey of the chosen district, finding out which villages already have churches of any denomination. He takes an ecumenical approach and would only go to those without a church. He would ask the senior church leader in the district, in this case an area dean or archdeacon, whether they would support starting churches in these villages. He would also contact neighbouring denominations to let them know about the evangelism and gain their support. Usually they had no objections and often welcomed the provision of a variety of churches in a district. After receiving encouragement to go ahead he would then recruit a team from the district to help with the evangelism.

All this brings the institutional dimension of church growth to the centre of attention. If a church is to grow across a district or a diocese it requires a strategic approach, with prioritizing, planning, budgeting, project management and ecumenical cooperation. The evangelist does this by consulting church leaders and working out where there are gaps. He plans how to fill these gaps most effectively, using the resources that are available to him locally. So a dimension of growth that may seem less important to the pastor, and of no interest to the new

Christian, is here placed alongside the others as an important part of the total picture.

To illustrate this, the director explained that he would take two months to start six churches in the designated villages. He would begin by asking the area dean or archdeacon and other pastors to nominate a group of people with recognizable spiritual gifts to be evangelists. He would then organize a seminar to train them how to preach about salvation and how to work under the local clergy. Then with his new team he would begin his visits to the villages, spending a week in each, working his way around the six, with a break in the middle.

What is interesting in all this is the contextualization of the strategy: he was not bringing a team in from a distant regional town or even from neighbouring districts but using people of the same ethnic group as those who were being evangelized. He explained that his team would usually be of younger people who were themselves fairly new to the Christian faith and still filled with their initial enthusiasm about it. While they may not have extensive knowledge of the Bible and doctrine they were nominated because others recognized their spiritual energy and wisdom. These were the best people to communicate the faith to non-believers because they themselves had been in that state not so very long ago. As Akiri has argued, lay ministers are key.

Another aspect of preparation for the evangelist was looking at the culture of the people he was seeking to reach, in order to work out how to present the gospel, and what if anything should be opposed in that culture. He quickly saw that aspects of the culture of many tribes, including these Kuria people of north-western Tanzania, were harmful, especially to children, girls and women. This is partly due to the traditional custom of giving and receiving dowry (bride price) and with FGM practised in many villages in Tarime and Serengeti districts in Mara region. His presentation would need to be appropriately tailored to these people, including clear condemnation of what was against the gospel message. In other words, some reflection on the nature of the gospel in this cultural setting was needed.

His analysis of Kuria culture also showed him that what he called a 'roadshow approach' to evangelism, where the people are invited to come and see what the church was offering and make up their own minds, would not be enough. Instead he believed he needed to use a 'spiritual approach', based on prayer and prayerful preaching and so calling upon divine help: 'Circumcision is spiritual paganism, so add the good news to transform their mindset.' This recalls the pastor's approach above, where he would sing a worship song and pray in the home of those he was visiting, calling on divine assistance, before challenging traditional practices like FGM.

This is important because it moderates the strategic approach described above. It shows that evangelism is not just about having an appropriate institutional strategy for starting churches. It requires something more: an incorporation of the strategy within a bigger arena of spiritual conflict between the powers of God and the powers of darkness. Prayer is needed to invoke divine assistance to challenge and overturn the grip of harmful practices in the pagan culture. The evangelism, in other words, is not just about conveying information about the gospel to those listening: it also includes somehow bringing that gospel *into effect* in the lives of those being evangelized, a sacramental dimension.

In the wider Mara region, and indeed in much of Tanzania, the first contact with a village would be through one individual or family known to the pastor or the lay minister. Then that individual or family would introduce the visitor(s) to the elected government leaders, a civil servant, and in some but rare cases traditional elders, to inform them about the intention of starting a church. At this point it has proven to be very helpful that many have already heard of the Anglican Church through its community projects, one of the most high-profile in this district being its campaign against FGM, through the opening of a safe house and educational work out in the villages. Another has been its support for victims of HIV and AIDS, and a third is its provision of schools in the region. These projects have benefited their communities in their own right, and have also generated goodwill and openness to Anglican evangelism. In many villages the elders have said, 'We need the Anglican church to come here.' This reinforces the community service dimension of church growth already noted in the pastor's testimony above.

The approach in each village then follows a standard pattern. The team of ten arrives and sets up camp for a week. Some team members are pastors, including the one who lives nearest this village and who will become the pastor for this village. There will be open-air preaching in a central location over four afternoons. Then in the evenings they will show the Jesus film (an American film closely based on the gospel accounts and dubbed into the vernacular Swahili language). Follow-up visits to the homes of those who are showing interest will take place over the next three days (as in the pastor's account above), to provide basic teaching about the Christian faith. This will be done by members of the team in pairs, in the mornings after the showing of the film. At the end of the week the team will leave but return two weeks later to do any follow-up that is needed, especially some more home visits.

At this point the new Christians from the village are invited to choose their elders, ideally a mixed group of men and women, both old and young. This turns the group from being a collection of different people into being one body, what the director calls the 'church plant'. Under the supervision of the local pastor they begin their Christian journey together, reading and/or listening to their Bible, encouraging each other and praying together. In due course the pastor prepares them for baptism and then confirmation. Baptism will happen as soon as people are ready. The confirmation will wait for the bishop on his next visit to the area. At this point these villagers will become a eucharistic community recognized as a church in their own right within the wider parish and within the diocese at large.

This reinforces and adds detail to three of the dimensions of church growth already identified above. First, the entrusting of new Christians with choosing their elders and so with their formation into a church plant is a magnificent vote of confidence in them. They are being empowered with ownership of their own life as a body of believers. This shows a quality of respect being integral to church growth and illustrates how this form of evangelism is appropriately described as 'community evangelism'.

Second, the evangelist's approach contains an explicitly sacramental dimension to what is happening, 'sacramental' as in 'of the sacraments'. For the sacraments of baptism, confirmation and the Eucharist have an acknowledged and important place in the whole.

Third, it is important to note how the evangelism is incorporated within the wider life of the neighbouring parish and diocese. The new Christians will not be left on their own – they are to become part of a wider structure and be supported by that structure through the local pastor. This shows good corporate organization behind the public evangelistic meetings and the home visiting, an organization structured to support and sustain the new Christians in their future life as a church. Once again, the evangelism is shown to have a communal dimension.

I asked the evangelist which aspect of the week-long campaign usually has the most impact on the villagers. He reported that it is the Jesus film, and especially its portrayal of Jesus' crucifixion. This can make people cry. It is the fact that Jesus was beaten and put to death even though he was innocent, and that he was doing this on behalf of everyone else. Some of the villagers are converted there and then.

I pressed him further and asked him why this was so. He replied that the film's portrayal of the crucifixion is an 'entry point' for the Christian faith to penetrate the lives and culture of those people. In their traditional culture they have been a fighting people who have frequently waged war on neighbouring villages and tribes. But they also have long-established ways of bringing about reconciliation with their neighbours, for example through slaughtering a lamb and using its blood for the joint washing of their hands, as a sign of making peace.

So when in the film they see Jesus shedding his blood on the cross to bring about reconciliation between us and God, this makes profound sense. Furthermore, the reconciliation ritual also includes having a meal together, eating the meat of the slaughtered lamb. This means that the symbolism of Holy Communion, in which the body and blood of the Lamb of God are eaten by the communicants, also makes sense and strikes a deep chord: they quickly understand what it is about.

All this strongly reinforces two other dimensions of evangelism identified in the pastor's testimony. First, it highlights the role of effective communication, not just through preaching but through other media such as film (when appropriately dubbed into the local vernacular language) and through conversation within the home. The communication not only conveys the message verbally but illustrates it with a vivid and gripping film, engaging the enquirer in discussion at their own level and in their own culturally appropriate way.

Second, the 'entry point' makes an important connection between an aspect of traditional culture – the ritual of reconciling with an enemy – and of being reconciled with God through the blood of Christ on the cross. Becoming a Christian, then, is not just about joining a group of people who sing and pray together; it has a key inner dimension, which is the personal forgiveness and reconciliation of the believer with their God, so being enabled to follow Christ as his disciple for the rest of their lives. The initiation of discipleship is an important dimension of what takes place in the campaign.

The director of evangelism in Mara Diocese finished by saying with excitement: 'The district is opening up to the gospel. Many are becoming Christians and the church is spreading from village to village.'

There is an additional element to all this that was mentioned by the recently retired bishop of Mara Diocese, Hilkiah Omindo. It concerns the long-term companionship link between this diocese and Leeds Diocese (previously Wakefield) in the north of England. This has been in place since 1988 and includes around 60 parish-to-parish links, with support for primary and secondary education, water and farming development, health care, visits in both directions and much else. He reported that in the 30 years he was diocesan bishop these links and friendship have instilled a sense of confidence in the parishes of his diocese: Anglicans there have known that they are not alone, that others in another part of the world remember and pray for them and they stand 'bega kwa bega' (shoulder to shoulder) with them (the Swahili phrase has become the motto of the whole relationship). This is not a donor–recipient relationship but one where the connection of friendship is primary and any practical support is a secondary by-product of that relationship. Bishop Hilkiah explained that Mara Anglicans have felt able to reach into new villages and create new churches and projects because they knew they had the ongoing backing of prayer and support from their friends in England and other parts of the world.

This comment shows that part of the quality of the community life that surrounds and supports the evangelism comes from a wider connectedness. The churches of the diocese are not free-standing and self-contained units but have a wider set of relationships that connect them to something bigger, which is not just the wider parish or diocese but a global network of friendship and support. The maintaining and valuing of this on both sides strengthens the confidence of the churches to reach out in local evangelism and church growth.

2

What, then, is Church Growth?

Different Dimensions of Growth

The ordinands, pastor and Mara director of evangelism, with further guidance from Mwita Akiri, have provided a set of textured and complementary accounts of the remarkable church growth that is taking place in their dioceses. It is now time to draw together from their accounts a summary of the various dimensions of church growth and provide some commentary on what has been happening. This will provide an overview that will then become a staging post for some more detailed analysis in the next section of the book, on what the stages of church growth might be, in order to gain a clearer linear view of its development through time. As this analysis is undertaken we will be returning at various points to the question asked at the start of this book, about whether 'Mara growth' could be expressed in a different context such as in contemporary Britain.

The first dimension of growth, and perhaps the most obvious, though it was explicitly mentioned only by the director of evangelism, is the numerical growth of the church. This was planned for in the evangelist's initial strategic analysis and in the integration of his programme within wider parochial, diocesan and ecumenical structures. It was deliberately sought in a methodical moving from village to village, over a two-month period or quarterly or, in the case of the pastor, more frequent open-air preaching. It was consolidated in the careful incorporation of new congregations into existing support structures of parish and diocese. What is distinctive is that this numerical growth was not measured in the number of individual conversions but in the number of new congregations. This shows a communal approach to evangelism in which the spread of the Christian faith is sought through multiplication of congregational communities rather than just individual membership or attendance figures, moving away from an individualistic to a corporate perspective. But the overriding feature in all this is that growth has a clear institutional dimension, which is expressed in measurable enlargement.

Akiri adds:

One has to remember that during the 1970s, Julius Nyerere, the first President of Tanzania and the Father of the Nation, reorganized rural settlements into what was known as Ujamaa villages. 'Ujamaa' can be roughly translated as 'familyhood'. These were settlements of varying sizes in terms of area and population, ranging from 3,000 to 5,000 people. The purpose was to facilitate the provision of social services such as school and dispensaries and infrastructure such as earth roads, and maximize the potential of people by engaging, for example, in communal farm and construction activities.

The existence of these organized rural settlements has facilitated the work of evangelism, not only in Mara region but the whole of Tanzania. They have made it easier for preachers and evangelism teams to organize open-air preaching and share the good news with the people in their homes, and have contributed to the numerical growth we see. In this way, their presence is a gift to churches even today, along with Nyerere's understanding of everyone as brother or sister, or 'ndugu' in Kiswahili, which has taken away much if not all hostility towards the pastor or lay minister when they visit homes in the village.

But was numerical growth the primary purpose of 'Mara growth'? Recent literature on church growth has argued that numerical growth needs to be given much more prominence in the practice of mission. For example, *Towards a Theology of Church Growth,* a set of wide-ranging and informative essays edited by David Goodhew (2015) on the biblical roots, theology and history of church growth, helpfully brings the concept of numerical growth to prominence within missiological debate, showing that it is a dimension of church growth that needs to have a more prominent place at the table. The accounts from Tanzania have nuanced this, however, and suggested that it should not be the primary *aim* of the enterprise. At no point did any of those who were interviewed indicate that the purpose of what they were doing was to increase the size of the institution. Instead they made it clear that their aim was to evangelize on the basis of good relationships. This was seen in the fostering of respectful relationships between the evangelists and interested villagers and between the villagers themselves when they came to faith. There was a noticeable absence of coercion in the preaching and home visiting, with an emphasis on enquirers having a choice of whether to respond or not. Those who wanted to learn more had been visited in their own homes and given time to ask questions and learn about the Christian faith. This represented a significant investment of time by the evangelists: more people could have been contacted in other ways but the quality of the contact would have been less good, with less opportunity to listen to the views and questions of the enquirers and to respond in appropriate and sensitive ways. This shows deep respect and the building of personal trust – going for quality not quantity, as it were.

Furthermore, the description above of how new Christians are empowered to elect their own elders and to form their own church also showed a high level of respect and trust. The willingness of congregations to start new congregations nearer to where people lived also showed priority being given to new Christians' needs over the convenience of the current congregation. Finally, the holding and valuing of long-term companionship links with an overseas diocese and between their respective parishes showed a valuing of ongoing relationship at a global level as well.

Related to this, an interactive form of evangelism was at the heart of the enterprise. There were two aspects to this: on the one hand, both the pastor and evangelist communicated a clear and definite message about the sovereignty of God in creation and of the gospel of Christ, which also included a direct challenging of some aspects of the local culture, such as FGM. This was complemented by showing the Jesus film, giving a complete account of Jesus' life, ministry, death and resurrection. But on the other hand this was all done in a way that the villagers could engage with: the film was shown in the Kiswahili vernacular, bringing some to tears and conversion; the teaching was communicated using different media and crucially included an interactive dimension through conversations in enquirers' homes in which the message could be explained through questions and answers in the most appropriate way for those people.

At several points in the accounts the development of a sacramental expression of the gospel was also apparent. This was seen in the way the actual sacraments of baptism, confirmation and communion were incorporated into the whole process, with communion creatively related to a traditional reconciliation meal within Kuria culture.

Akiri continues:

Kuria culture puts emphasis on the rite of passage, especially male and female circumcision, to make a transition from childhood to adulthood. Female circumcision is dehumanizing and is a case of gender violence; male circumcision in the bush is discouraged. Yet when Kuria Christians come to baptism they view it as some kind of childhood rite, with confirmation providing entry into proper adulthood. Equally, participation in communion is seen as a seal of inclusion and acceptance into a community. This is why most Kuria people subsequently regard excommunication from church and from Holy Communion as a serious sign of rejection (if and when it happens).

But worship more generally, especially worship with choirs and dance using a PA system broadcasting the music to the neighbourhood, was seen to be sacramental, not just describing salvation but allowing a kind of active participation within it, allowing the Spirit to move in the hearts and limbs of the worshippers.

Making connections with the church's service of the wider community was another important element within the mix. While community projects were not undertaken to convert people (whether these involved training farmers, water projects, campaigning against FGM, or nursery education in churches), they were regarded as part of the overall 'holistic' nature of Christian mission. They attracted villagers wanting to find out more, preparing the ground for evangelism, and came to be seen by many as expressing an important aspect of what the Christian faith is all about – God's care for them – so opening their hearts and lives to the possibility of faith.

Finally, the accounts drew attention to the nurturing of discipleship in evangelism. They described how villagers would need to choose to repent and be reconciled with God, how they would then be freed from inner fear of subjection to evil and from dangers of witchcraft, to be brought into the security of God's kingdom. This personal dimension of the whole process was especially helped by evangelism taking place in the home and so gaining direct application to family life. In some of the testimonies the home environment was where crucial interaction with the gospel took place and where the foundations of lifelong discipleship were laid.

Overall, then, the interviews and analysis from Tanzania have revealed no fewer than *six* dimensions of church growth; alongside numerical growth there has been growth of congregational relationships, growth of interactive evangelism, an increasing dynamism of sacramental life, a strengthening of community service, and a nurturing of personal discipleship. Each dimension has been seen to be integral to the whole, showing a rich interconnectedness to what was happening. In terms of the way the growth has actually unfolded in the villages, it can be summed up as growth that is rooted in community service, led by an interactive evangelism; this includes sacramental expression, with deeply respectful congregational relationships, and bearing fruit in discipleship and institutional enlargement. The accounts from Mara, then, have revealed a complex ecology of growth.

An Ecclesiology of Growth

What is the wider significance of all this? Can it speak to and contribute to ongoing theological discussion of the nature of the church and of church growth? To begin to answer this we need to locate the approach within contemporary ecclesiology. One accessible and systematic way of doing this is to draw on Avery Dulles' widely influential survey of ecclesiology in his *Models of the Church* (first published 1974, expanded edition 1987) and compare the above with his schema. How do the accounts from Tanzania correlate with this, and what does it suggest about them?

Dulles presented 'a critical analysis of the church in all its aspects', in which he summarized the results of his analysis of recent major writings on the nature of the church and 'sifted out five major approaches, types, or, as I prefer to call them, models'. He considered and evaluated each in turn, providing illuminating pen portraits with revealing quotations from both Catholic and Protestant writings. He also wrote, revealingly, that:

> as a result of this critical assessment I draw the conclusion that a balanced theology of the Church must find a way of incorporating the major affirmations of each basic ecclesiological type. Each of the models calls attention to certain aspects of the Church that are less clearly brought out by the other models. (Dulles 1987, p. 9)

It is important to add that in the second edition of the book he added a sixth model which had recently come to prominence, and this is included here.

What, then, are his models and how do they connect with church growth in Mara region? The first model presents the church as 'institution': 'Throughout its history, from the very earliest years, Christianity has always had an institutional side. It has had recognized ministers, accepted confessional formulas, and prescribed forms of public worship' (Dulles 1987, p. 35). This model therefore views the church as a corporate body existing through human history, with formal structures of membership, leadership, delivery and account-ability. Like other institutions it is quantifiable and therefore its component parts can be counted, such as in the number of congregations, of members and of attendance at services. When the Mara director of evangelism, or a priest or a lay minister, plans their evangelistic strategy, and works their way around an area with the purpose of increasing the number of congregations, they are operating out of this model of church life, bringing its assumptions and frameworks to bear for monitoring and assessing what they are doing.

But 'Mara growth' also placed a strong emphasis on building up good relationships with the wider community and within the new congregation. This relates to Dulles' second model, which views the church as a community, of both human and divine persons, a 'mystical communion'. This operates through personal association, intimacy, mutual participation in prayer, a fusion of people in a divine common life, through sympathy and mutual identification, for which 'we' is the natural expression (Dulles 1987, p. 48). A high level of respect and personal freedom is fundamental to this view. It expresses a dimension of church life that is not quantifiable and therefore cannot be counted. Instead it is concerned above all with the quality of relationships within the fellowship. From scripture the images of the church as the body of Christ, and as the people of God, especially harmonize with this model (p. 50).

Dulles' third model is drawn from the writings of the French Catholic theologian Henri de Lubac:

If Christ is the sacrament of God, the Church is for us the sacrament of Christ; she represents him, in the full and ancient meaning of the term, she really makes him present. She not only carries on his work, but she is his very continuation, in a sense far more real than that in which it can be said that any human institution is its founder's continuation. (Dulles 1987, p. 63)

The model of the church as 'sacrament' captures the way that the practices of the church, whether in worship or community life, or in the case of 'Mara growth' in preaching, singing and dancing, and the use of actual sacraments, do not just convey information about Christ but in tangible ways convey the gift of his presence into the lived experience of those who participate in them. They are effective signs of what they proclaim, the coming together of human and divine action. The church as a whole embodies this divine gift in human form but these sacramental moments bring that larger reality into specific tangible experience. In particular they give church growth its living beating heart. Dulles helpfully elaborates these key points:

Consistent with this point of view, *Lumen gentium* [of the Second Vatican Council] in Article 3 asserts that the Church is the Kingdom of heaven now present in mystery. In other words, the Church is here described as the mystery or sacramental presence of the ultimate, consummated Kingdom. In this ecclesiology, therefore, the church is seen as eschatological insofar as it is a sacrament of the eschatological Kingdom. The sacrament is in the first place a sign. By its visible presence the Church reminds men of God's Kingdom and keeps alive their hope for the blessings of eternal life.

Crucially he then adds:

But it is more than a sign. It betokens the actual presence, in a hidden way, of that to which it points. What is essential to the Kingdom, the reconciling grace of Christ, is truly at work in the Church, although not exclusively in the Church. The Church, with the help of the gospel and of the Holy Spirit, is able to discern and celebrate the gifts of God to men. It assembles in manifest visibility about the altar of the Lord and proclaims the Lord's death until he comes. At the Eucharist the Church becomes more than ever a sacramental sign of the heavenly Jerusalem. (Dulles 1987, p. 114)

But in Mara this sacramentality was associated less with the Eucharist and more with a clear and forceful communication of the gospel in words. Evangelists and lay ministers would preach in the public square of the village and not be afraid to challenge the traditional beliefs of the villagers with the gospel message. This corresponds with Dulles' fourth model, of the church as 'herald'. In this view the word is primary and the sacrament secondary:

It sees the Church as gathered and formed by the word of God. The mission of the Church is to proclaim that which it has heard, believed, and been commissioned to proclaim ... [and vis-à-vis the second model] it emphasizes faith and proclamation over interpersonal relationships and mystical communion. (Dulles 1987, p. 76)

Dulles connects this model with the work of Karl Barth, in which the concept of the Word of God plays a central part in his *Church Dogmatics*, becoming for many its defining characteristic. Dulles then illustrates this model vividly: the 'basic image is that of the herald of a king who comes to proclaim a royal decree in a public square' (Dulles 1987, p. 76). So the emphasis is on the church as a purveyor of a message that needs to be relayed to the wider community in the most educationally effective ways. What is interesting in Mara's evangelism is that this is done both through public proclamation and also through interactive conversation in the intimacy of an enquirer's home. It again shows the communitarian bias of this whole approach.

But not everything that the church does is geared towards evangelism. As already noted, in Tanzania the dioceses run a range of impressive projects to equip and support subsistence farmers, those afflicted by HIV/AIDS, those without access to clean water, girls escaping FGM and the young needing education.

Akiri continues:

Credit goes to the nineteenth-century missionary societies, the Universities' Mission to Central Africa on the Anglo-Catholic side and the Church Missionary Society (UK and Australia) on the Evangelical side, for making community projects an integral part of their missionary work from the very beginning when they commenced their work halfway through that century in Tanzania. Circumstances and the environment for engaging in community development projects may have changed today yet there is a theological basis for such an engagement (cf. Matthew 14.13–21; 25.35–40; Luke 10.25–37) and the legacy of these missionary societies lives on.

This community service relates closely to Dulles' fifth model, the church as 'servant'. He quotes Dietrich Bonhoeffer, writing from his Nazi prison cell, for a description of this model. Bonhoeffer called for a change of attitude to the world on the part of the churches. This call became a key influence in establishing the popularity of the 'servant' model of the church:

The Church is the Church only when it exists for others. To make a start, it should give away all its property to those in need. The clergy must live solely on the free-will offerings of their congregations, or possible engage in some secular calling. The Church must share in the secular problems of ordinary human life, not dominating, but helping and serving. (Dulles 1987, pp. 94–5, quoting from Bonhoeffer 1971, pp. 203–4)

So the church was not to bring the world under its own authority, but to serve the human needs of its people. It was not to be just interested in the size of the institution or the quality of its own community life or of its communication, but to have a keen commitment to making a positive impact on the lives of those in need. The dioceses of Mara region illustrate this model in many ways, showing what might be termed a holistic approach to mission, addressing the needs of the body as well as the soul.

Dulles' sixth and final model is of the church as a 'community of disciples'. The emphasis here is back on the quality of the church community itself, but unlike in the second model it is not so much a concern for the quality of the relationships in themselves as about the faithfulness of their discipleship, in growing to spiritual maturity as followers of Christ, both when they meet together and in their home and working lives. This model 'precludes the impression that ecclesial communion exists merely for the sake of mutual gratification and support. It calls attention to the ongoing relationship of the Church to Christ, its Lord, who continues to direct it through his Spirit' (Dulles 1987, p. 206). In 'Mara growth' it is seen in the emphasis on personal repentance and commitment to Christ and joining with others in their ongoing Christian lives as members of the church, as elders and evangelists. It is seen in the taking of responsibility for the life of the church expressed in a widely used slogan of being 'self-extending, self-supporting and self-governing'.

This multiple correspondence with Dulles' highly regarded survey of ecclesiology shows that what has been happening in Mara region is not an oddity with little relevance to the wider church but rather an example, albeit a distinctive and vivid one, of the wider multi-faceted nature of the Catholic church. Furthermore, it adds to Dulles' account because it shows what his theoretical portrait looks like in the context of the global South, where the church is growing healthily. It especially shows the leading role of evangelism within the multi-dimensional nature of the church, but an evangelism rooted in the community life of the congregation and in its relationship with its surrounding community.

Building on this dialogue with Dulles, how can all these models or dimensions of growth be viewed as a whole? We need an analogy that captures their diversity in unity in a memorable image. From what has been reported from Tanzania it should not be an image of an instrumental or mechanical process, in which certain steps inevitably produce expected quantifiable outcomes. This kind of process has a place in the whole, when viewing the church as an institution, but it is very far from being the whole. When the transforming of human relationships, with each other and with God, is at the centre of what is happening, then qualitative rather than quantitative factors are in play. Some other broader and deeper image of growth is needed.

At this point we can take a lead from the apostle Paul, who in 1 Corinthians 3.6 writes: 'I planted, Apollos watered, but God gave the growth.' This suggests an organic analogy for church growth, such as the growth of a great oak tree in its relationships with its environment. One dimension of that growth is an enlargement in the size of the tree, in its height and width, which can be measured year on year. But there are other dimensions, such as how it grows down into the ground through its root system, the way it grows within its trunk and individual branches, strengthening their capacity to carry the weight of the canopy, and the fact that it grows in its capacity to provide a home to other creatures such as birds, squirrels and insects. In the same way, as we have seen, church growth takes place in a variety of ways, in different dimensions, centred on a variety of patterns of human relationship within the church and between the church and the wider community – a complex ecology of growth.

Furthermore, the growth of an oak tree takes place through various kinds of ongoing interaction: at one moment taking in elements of sunlight, rain, CO_2, nutrients, at another moment giving out oxygen, leaves, acorns, shelter. There is an ongoing movement in two directions arising out of the tree being a living and breathing organism. This image corresponds very well with Dulles' own fine summary of his models, one of the concluding passages in his book:

> The Church is never more Church ... than when it gathers for instruction and worship. On such occasions it becomes most palpably the 'sacrament of Christ' as proposed in the third model. But it would not be completely Church unless it went forth from its assemblies to carry on Christ's work in the world. The Church's existence is a continual alternation between two phases. Like systole and diastole in the movement of the heart, like inhalation and exhalation in the process of breathing, assembly and mission succeed each other in the life of the Church. Discipleship would be stunted unless it included both the centripetal phase of worship and the centrifugal phase of mission. Mission, in turn, implies both evangelization and service, the foci of the fourth and fifth ecclesiological models. (Dulles 1987, p. 220)

This view of the church as, in essence, a two-directional movement is echoed and given biblical referencing by a recent and widely welcomed Church of England report on discipleship, *Setting God's People Free*:

> When we ask, 'What is the church? Who is the church? and Where is the church?' our answers should be framed by the lens of viewing the identity and purpose of the Church in the light of the missionary activity of God as it is constituted in the servant witness of Christ and in the outpourings of the Holy Spirit.
>
> Throughout Jesus' ministry the disciples are dispersed and gathered (Luke 9.1–6, and Luke 10.1–12), a pattern that continues after his death and resurrection in the form of the great commission to go and make disciples in the power of the Holy Spirit (Matthew 28.16–20; Mark 16.14–18; Luke 24.44–53; John 20.21–22; Acts 1.6–11). This dynamic of 'gathering' and 'sending' forms a dialectical relationship

within the one church as it participates in the redemptive activity of God. (Church of England 2017, 1.4)

What, then, is church growth within such a dynamic conception? As is now clear, it cannot just be an increase in the size of the gathered church viewed as a self-contained institution. This would be to distort the nature of the church. Instead, both directions of movement must be taken into account: church growth needs to be seen as an increase in the reach and scope of that movement, in the extent of both gathering and dispersing. It is, in other words, all about an increase in interaction with its surrounding community in which neither side loses itself but in which both build up purposeful and life-giving relationships. The organic analogy works well here: it points to the way a tree interacts with its environment, drawing what it needs from that environment and bringing life and health to those organisms and creatures that pass beneath it or shelter in its branches or breathe the oxygen that it generates. We have seen this movement taking place in a number of ways: through its people growing in community relationships, in the flourishing of their sacramental life, in the strengthening of their evangelistic communication, in the extension of their community service, in the extending and deepening of their discipleship, and through institutional growth. Each of these is integral to the whole, showing a rich interconnectedness in its ecology that ultimately depends on the life that God in Christ through his Spirit gives it, which is like the sap rising through the tree and reaching every branch, twig and leaf.

A number of tasks arise out of the use of this analogy. The first is to unpack it in more detail, especially to identify the main *stages* of growth within each dimension of growth. This requires some closer analysis of the interviews and other reports from Mara region and then, when the respective stages are clear, to identify examples in other contexts to establish how this framework is of general relevance to the wider church, and this is undertaken in the next chapter. Then in the following chapter the framework as a whole is compared and contrasted with other views of church growth, to see which of them provides the most comprehensive perspective. To help church leaders move from these theoretical considerations to the practice of ministry, practical principles for church growth are distilled out of this discussion. Finally, an example is provided in the last main chapter of what this can look like in a British context, putting flesh and blood on these theoretical bones.

3

Stages of Growth

While church growth in Mara region has been most dramatic in the new churches it has also taken place in some of the older churches. I was shown this when interviewing an elderly ordinand at the Bible college. A gaunt and serious figure, his manner of speaking was slower and more deliberate than that of his younger peers, using a form of the Queen's English from an earlier era. When he said he wanted to tell me about his home church, which had started in 1952, I was sceptical: would he be able to add anything to the story of new young churches springing up in Mara today? But his story rebuked my scepticism because it was a story of mature growth.

He told me of how the church began with eight members who were mostly from one family, that of the local chief. It met in his home compound. He had originally come to faith through contact with lay catechists from Kenya, men who had crossed the border and walked down the shore of Lake Victoria from the north, preaching and starting churches as they went. Their brand of Christianity was known as 'CMS', reflecting its origins in the work of the Church Missionary Society in Kenya earlier in the century. The first church they started in Mara region was at Kowak, which is now the cathedral parish of the new diocese of Rorya. The chief's church, at Buhemba in Musoma district, began life shortly after that. The ordinand told me how it attracted new members from different tribal groups: the chief was a Zanaki but he struck up a friendship with a Luo teacher at the local primary school, who came to worship at his church. Then, when a gold mine opened nearby, drawing other Luos to the area, some of them also joined the church. This showed that it had made an important transition, from being a kinship group to being a body able to accept newcomers on an equal footing – a growth in maturity.

The congregation increased in size and in 1974 decided to change its name from 'CMS' to 'Anglican'. This was controversial and not supported by everyone, but it showed the church wanting to connect deliberately and formally with recently established national and diocesan church structures in Tanzania, where the Anglican Church of Tanzania was now constituted, rather than continue as an outpost of a missionary society's work from a neighbouring country. This also demonstrated a maturing of relationships, this time with the outside church, moving from a donor–recipient type of relationship to one of partnership with other parishes in a diocesan structure. At this point the parish was able to send two of its members to be trained as pastors, a gift to the wider church and a further sign of maturity.

Partnership with the world church became a reality in 1974 when an agriculturalist from New Zealand moved to the area to open a farm development centre. He brought funding to do this and the centre has since helped to bring significant improvements to farming techniques in the surrounding district. It is now owned and operated by the local diocese, who work in partnership with international NGOs on various projects. But the agriculturalist was also an Anglican and became a member of the church. He was able to assist the congregation in the construction and extending of their church building.

Population levels in the area fluctuated and with that the size of the congregation. At its height it was attracting between 700 and 800 every Sunday, with over 1,000 on special feast days. The arrival of other churches in the area also reduced the weekly attendance to some degree, and so the story is not one of simple growth in one direction. Today the regular congregation fluctuates between 200 and 400, with a Sunday school of around 200 children and 50–70 young people in the choir, supported by a PA system. There are plans to establish a chicken project and, when the rains come, cultivation of the church field to grow cash crops. Furthermore, another of the ordinands at the college, a young woman who is a gifted singer, described how this church had organized evangelism in a neighbouring village, which had resulted in a new church starting there. This church currently had a congregation of between 50 and 60, with a reader and an evangelist, and was attracting new members.

What I heard from the ordinands, then, was the story of a church that had gradually grown to maturity over the years and was faithfully serving its area, responding to the spiritual needs of its people in relevant ways at different times. Sometimes this yielded very large congregations and at other times, owing to factors outside its control, smaller ones. Numerical size, in other words, was not the barometer of its health and growth. Other less visible factors were at play, to do with the quality of relationships within the congregation and between the congregation and the wider community, its capacity to nurture discipleship, the quality of its worship and its commitment to evangelism.

All of this therefore highlights the need to map out clearly the stages of growth, from birth to maturity, in all six dimensions. The story of Buhemba in Musoma district has shown that the launch of a church is not its completion, like the production of a new car rolling off a production line. It is more like the growth of a tree, an organic process that takes place throughout its life, from germination all the way through to maturity, in different ways at different times.

The organic analogy provides some helpful orientation as we begin to identify stages of church growth. It points to the way growth in the natural world, such as with a tree, takes place through a number of stages not defined by fixed periods of time but by qualitative differences. A tree begins its life as a seed germinating in the ground. This may take only a few hours. It grows into a tender sapling, over the course of a few days or weeks and then after a year or two becomes a young tree. Finally, in its own time, it gradually stretches up and out to become a mature tree with a complex ecology, which can take decades. Similarly, church growth will not take place in fixed and measurable units or periods of time, to be measured like a person's height or age, but in different qualitative stages of uneven periods.

What, then, does the case study reveal about these stages? For the sake of consistency, in order to allow for comparison between different types of growth, three stages will be identified within each dimension. This subdivision is logical in that in each case it allows for the identification of where growth starts, what happens in the middle, and where it ends up. Crucially, it allows consistent mapping of the whole, with three common points of comparison throughout.

Institutional Growth

Beginning with the growth of the institution itself, stages of growth can be revealed using some insights from organizational studies, especially the work of Helen Cameron who has charted the different forms of organization found within different kinds of churches. She writes that organizational form 'can be defined as the legal ownership and constitution under which an organization operates' (Cameron and Marashi 2004, p. 5, quoted in Cameron 2010, pp. 40–1). She presents five different forms, which range in structure from simple to complex. The first is what she calls the 'public utility' form, which are churches constituted to provide a service to the whole community; second is the 'voluntary association' form, which are churches constituted by and for a voluntary membership; third is the 'network' form, which are churches formed by their members for a specific networking purpose (a variation of the voluntary association); fourth is the 'friendship group' form, which are informal gatherings of friends or acquaintances who meet regularly for worship; and fifth is the 'third-place meeting' form, which are churches that meet in another organization's premises and with their support, such as in coffee shops or hospitals or gyms, so do not need to become fully autonomous organizations.

Cameron does not intend the different forms to reveal different stages of church growth: they are simply different ways of being a church and none are superior to any of the others. But when studying actual churches it is possible to trace characteristic patterns of development from one type to another, and it is these patterns that are being identified here. As we shall see, three of these forms can be identified in Mara region. Their appearance there, and the way there is often development from one to the next, is a revealing example of institutional growth through three clear stages (though remembering that one is not somehow superior to the next, in the same way that an adult is not somehow superior to a child). This could throw light on the nature of church growth generally.

One of Cameron's forms, the friendship group form, is commonly found in Mara. This is a group of friends/acquaintances who meet on a regular basis to read and study the Bible, worship and pray together. The gathering is voluntary, informal and for mutual support. In the history of the church in the West it can be seen and validated from the Reformation period onwards. Martin Luther lays theological foundations for this when he describes how the following was sufficient to constitute a church:

Now, anywhere you hear or see [the Word of God] preached, believed, confessed, and acted upon, do not doubt that the true *ecclesia sancta catholica*, a 'holy Christian people' must be there, even though there are very few of them ... And even if there were no other sign than this alone, it would be enough to prove that a holy Christian people must exist there, for God's word cannot be without God's people, and conversely, God's people cannot be without God's word. (*On the Councils and the Church*, in McGrath 1999, pp. 202–3)

Whenever a group of people meet in this unincorporated kind of way, the church is present.

This form can be detected in Mara region when a new church is formed. As we have heard, villagers who respond to evangelism are gathered into their own informal group. They begin their life together by reading the Bible, praying and encouraging each other in their faith. This practice resembles what the first converts were doing in the early church (Acts 2.42–47). They are responsible for their church life and are encouraged to choose those who will lead it as elders. They receive support from an outside pastor but he does not own or control their church – they are self-determining. This is therefore a friendship group: their life together is based on their friendship with Christ and each other. To a great extent, this is facilitated by a strong sense of familyhood and the need to belong that is still found in African societies, which create bonds in communities.

After a certain period of time, however, when teaching has taken place and the sacraments of baptism, confirmation and the Eucharist have become part of their life, this informal group of Christians is formally constituted into a church in its own right by the diocese. It starts to be governed by a set of procedures received from the diocese including a membership list and the possibility of having their own pastor. All this corresponds with another of Cameron's forms, the voluntary association. In this form, not necessarily better but certainly different, a group puts in place structured ways of organizing its life that do not depend on ties of friendship or acquaintance, normally through adopting a constitution with a formal membership list for those who choose to join. The voluntary association has definite membership, set procedures for members to run the association themselves and an agreed aim. Churches that operate in this kind of structure can grow to be larger than friendship groups because they do not need to depend on a specific kinship group – as happened in Buhemba. Their membership gathers for worship or other activities on the basis of formal membership in an organized way, so they are gathered congregations.

The Congregationalism of Robert Browne (c.1550–1633) is one of the earliest examples of this kind of Christian voluntary association in the English-speaking world. In 1582, during the reign of Elizabeth I, he showed how this kind of church was different from a geographically based parish church: 'The Kingdom of God was not to be begun by whole parishes, but rather of the worthiest, were they never so few' (Brown 2013, p. 404). He insisted that these gathered churches of the 'worthiest', bound under God by covenant, should be independent of the state and have the right to govern themselves. Such separatist principles became the 'congregationalism' of those who followed him. The Pilgrim Fathers set sail for America in 1620 with members of a congregational church in Plymouth, Devon (as well as Puritans from Holland) to found Plymouth, Massachusetts, where they escaped the constraints of the Anglican establishment and the parish system in England. Today, across the Protestant world, this is now the most common form of church organization, including within the Anglican Communion.

One variant of this form are larger churches that have two or more gathered congregations, with the different types of worship that appeal to different groups within them. But the voluntarist principle of association is still fundamental to their form.

There is a third organizational form that is also widespread, especially in the Roman Catholic nations of Europe and within the Church of England. This form has a very different principle of membership, not one in which people opt into membership but one in which they and everyone else in a geographical area already have membership. This is sometimes called the community type of church, in which the church is identified with the wider community in a defined area, where it fulfils certain religious functions on the community's behalf. In Helen Cameron's terminology this kind of church is a public utility, providing an essential service (such as the rites of christening, marriage and burial), covering a geographical area, with no distinct membership but with legal officers to administer its functions (such as 'clerks in Holy Orders', to use the historic terminology of the Church of England).

An obvious example of this type is the traditional parish church of the Church of England, located at the heart of its geographical 'parish' district, and offering the rites of passage to anyone from that district who requests them. It forms a component part of the 'parish system' that goes back to medieval Christendom when it was widely established across Europe. But as populations have become more fluid and people have fewer ties to a geographical area they become less and less aware of their parish church, and it plays a decreasing role in their lives. Nevertheless, the system is still in place in England and its influence lives on in occasions like Remembrance Sunday when the parish church will often host the commemoration on behalf of the whole community.

One variant on this type are the 'greater churches' and cathedrals, which operate as public utilities in a range of ways, not least in the Christmas season when they provide carol services for community organizations and draw thousands of non-regular worshippers in through their doors. They host multiple communities from across their towns, cities and regions, including sometimes members of other faith communities.

What of Mara region? The Anglican Church is not legally established and has never had the kind of role the Church of England fulfils in relation to the state. Nor does it operate with a parish system in which the country is divided up into geographical parishes each with a designated parish church. There are large areas with no Anglican presence at all. Instead, as mentioned, churches generally operate as voluntary associations. They often call themselves parishes but by this they mean the people who gather to worship and who are formed into a church community. However, there are some signs of a community-wide calling in many churches, seen in the commitment to serve the physical and educational needs of the wider community through clinics, health programmes, water projects, nursery education during the week, farming development, and primary and secondary education. Most of this provision comes through the diocesan organization rather than individual churches, though the cathedral in the largest of the three dioceses provides significant support for orphans in its town. There are also churches in all three dioceses that support children through partnership with the Compassion International branches in Tanzania. Collectively, through its diocesan organizations, Anglican churches in Mara have taken on a version of the public utility form. While its provision of worship is mainly just for its members, its wider mission and especially its service to those in need is for everyone in the community who seeks it. As one of the bishops put it, 'People are attracted to the Anglican Church because it proclaims a holistic salvation, of the body as well as the soul. In particular, they see Anglican churches engaged in community and development projects as well as Sunday worship, and this is very appealing.' He is referring to wells that have been dug for village communities, a goat 'library' that operates to lend goats to families with HIV/AIDS who benefit from the nutritious milk, school classrooms in government schools that have been renovated, children's nurseries that have been opened, subsistence farmers who have been trained in irrigation and drought resistance and trees that have been planted.

Overall, then, the churches of Mara region show church growth taking place over time through three qualitative stages of growth. The first is illustrated by newly established churches in the recently evangelized areas, which meet informally for Bible study and prayer: these provide examples of the friendship group form of organization identified by Cameron. The second is illustrated in the majority of the diocese's churches, which are called parishes and are governed by a simple constitution with a defined membership: they provide examples of the more complex voluntary association form. The third is illustrated by the dioceses, acting on behalf of all the parishes, that have set up a range of projects for the wider community: it shows the church collectively taking on the public utility form, especially in relation to health care, development and education – a church that is learning to exist 'for the sake of those who are not its members', to adapt famous words often attributed to William Temple.

Examples of these three stages of growth can be identified in other contexts, showing how this framework can read what is happening around elsewhere. For example, the growth of informal friendship/acquaintanceship groups can be seen in the growth of 'fresh expressions of church'. Michael Moynagh, in his major study of the movement, *Church in Life*, which is discussed later in this chapter, provides this evocative description of the phenomenon:

> Something remarkable is happening in the Christianity of our times. The church is learning to express God's love in new ways. Across denominations and networks of churches, and sometimes outside them, in parts of Africa, Australia, Europe, North America and elsewhere, new ecclesial communities are popping up in the context of people's everyday lives in cafes, gyms, tattoo parlours, laundromats and even online games. This grassroots movement, if it really is a movement, is patchy, many communities are short-lived, and we still have a great deal to learn. But there is evidence of fruitfulness and gathering confidence in these communities' witness to the kingdom. (Moynagh 2017, p. 2)

As some of these new ecclesial communities become established they take on a more organized form, though many remain under the legal ownership and governance of their founding churches. Those that come to exist independently of parent churches often develop a defined membership and come to be governed by a constitution (which becomes a legal requirement). In this way they become like most other churches, which operate as voluntary associations, as we have already seen.

What of the transition from voluntary association to public utility? An immediate query is that for many churches in England the process of change has been in the opposite direction, from public utility form to voluntary association form. In response to growing secularization in society at large there has been a gradual reduction in attendances, which has resulted in parish churches, in particular, slowly losing their community-wide standing and becoming more congregationally focused. Clergy increasingly now minister to those who attend church rather than to the wider community. So the movement has been in a different direction from that in Mara. But does this invalidate the framework? Not necessarily: what it shows is that it is possible to move in either direction between voluntary association and public utility. Changes in circumstances can result in churches changing their form, in one direction or the other.

Organizational growth towards becoming a public utility, on the other hand, is illustrated by a more recent trend of churches starting up community projects, in a wide variety of forms, rediscovering a vocation to serve the communities in which they are placed. For example, in the report *Doing Good: A Future for Christianity in the 21st Century*, Nick Spencer argues that while the numbers of those attending church have continued to decline since 2006 research suggests that social action by Christians and churches has grown over the same period:

In so far as we have data to show for it, the level of [social action], both formally and informally, has risen considerably over the last ten years. There may be fewer people on pews but there are many more running luncheon clubs, and mums and toddlers groups, and foodbanks, and homeless charities, and debt-advice centres, and drop-in centres and the like. Christians are 'doing good'. (Spencer 2016, p. 12 and see further p. 45)

It is important to add that not all these churches would be perceived as public utilities by the community at large, so this point must not be overstated, but they do illustrate the start of a journey from the voluntary association form towards the public utility form, so giving expression to development from the second to the third stage of institutional growth described above. Overall, the report shows that this framework can be used to read and interpret what is happening here, at least for institutional growth.

Congregational Relationships

What of stages of growth in the quality of community relationships? From the case study it is possible to see three stages in
this dimension as well. The first is apparent when a new church
has just been launched in a village. At this point, as an informal
friendship group, the members are dependent on outside support. The visiting evangelism team has brought the good news
of the gospel, through village meetings, has shown the Jesus
film and engaged in home visiting. They have encouraged
the villagers to form themselves into a group that will meet
regularly, and they have arranged for the local pastor, from a
nearby parish, to come and teach them and prepare them for
baptism. The villagers themselves are required only to turn up,
with open minds and hearts, to read the Bible together, talk
to each other and pray together. Little formal commitment is
needed. They are recipients more than contributors, like young
people who at first depend entirely on what their parents provide. The new congregation is, essentially, at a receiving stage
in their community relationships, which is good and necessary
at this tender point in their life.

However, we have seen that quite early on in their life they
are asked to elect their own elders – those among them who
will coordinate their life and represent them to others. This is a
significant step because it shows the group taking responsibility
for their own life and therefore taking on a sense of ownership.
They will no longer just be recipients of what others are providing but become active participants in the shared endeavour of
becoming a church. This, as we have seen, shows the start of a
transition to the voluntary association form, where the church
takes on a constitution (however simple) with procedures for
enrolling new members and governing its internal life. As far as
the quality of community relationships is concerned, it shows a
transition from a donor–recipient form of relationship, where
the diocese through the evangelism team has been the donor
and they the recipient, to a partnership form of relationship,
where they contribute as much as they receive. They grow to

become 'self-extending, self-supporting, self-governing' within the support network of the diocese. Indeed, in due course, when they are fully constituted as a parish church in their own right, they will send representatives to help govern the diocese itself at its occasional synods.

But there is a third stage of growth pointed to by Dulles when he described the church as a 'mystical communion' of both divine and human persons. In 'Mara growth' this is seen when the interaction between the two parties, of the villagers and the diocese represented by the evangelism team, grows to acknowledge and consciously respond to a third party, which touches and connects them to something greater. Both the pastor and the director of evangelism described how they would begin their evangelism with prayer, either before the public meetings or at the start of a home visit. This would call upon God to be in the hearts and minds of all. When the villagers acknowledge and respond to this embrace, reaching out in faith and trust in their hearts and minds, they become active members of what is now a three-way relationship. God through his Spirit has been present from the beginning, but not necessarily recognized as such. Now all three parties are interacting with each other. So this third stage of relationship is all about God through the Holy Spirit being part of the community and connecting the villagers into his reality beyond their words and dialogue. It shows the Trinitarian dimension of church growth, that what goes on is not just between human agents but is caught up in the mission of God. The community of the church is constituted by divine as well as human persons: God in Christ acting through his Spirit in the hearts and minds of his people.

This third stage, which could start early in the life of a church, can also be identified in the singing and dancing when these activities touch and move those who are present. Music, of course, has the ability to affect people very deeply and when this is in the context of evangelism it can be the way that the third party in the mix, the Spirit of God, reaches into the hearts of people and converts them from within. This is why song and dance can sometimes become a sacrament of God's presence, an effective sign of his sovereign reality, and why they are so important in church growth.

The case study therefore reveals a pattern of growth in a congregation's relationships: from being essentially recipients in a donor–recipient relationship with those who have set it up – a one-way relationship – to becoming a partner of equal standing with others in a two-way partnership; and then, third, to finding and responding to the divine reality within these other relationships, which is the mystical community of the Trinity, a three-way relationship.

This interpretative framework can helpfully be used to uncover relationship dynamics in other contexts, for example the history of the relationship between Mara Diocese and its link Diocese of Wakefield (now part of Leeds Diocese). At the beginning of the link in 1988, Tanzania was a desperately poor country and Mara Diocese had next to no resources of its own. There were only a dozen parishes, some of which were struggling, and no diocesan infrastructure or resources, so everything had to be built from scratch. The connection with Wakefield Diocese was a lifeline, providing financial and material support for starting a diocese as well as for individual parishes. In practical terms it was clearly a donor–recipient kind of relationship, with the traffic mainly going in one direction – the first stage identified above.

As the link became more settled, a commitment was made on both sides to embody a certain philosophy at its heart, one summed up in the Swahili phrase 'bega kwa bega' (standing shoulder to shoulder). The people of the two dioceses were to become partners, supporting each other as far as possible, in a relationship of equals. This quickly became a reality in terms of praying for each other and in joint decision-making about how the link was to develop. It was harder to implement at local level, where parishes on both sides sometimes defaulted to a donor–recipient type of relationship. But overall it is possible to see a transition being made to the second stage of community relationship identified above.

Then, as the link became well established and groups travelled in both directions, the differences between the two sets of people – of language, culture, wealth, outlook – became less significant and the things that united them, their faith in Christ, discipleship, membership of the Anglican Communion, became more apparent. Furthermore, as they prayed together and shared each other's worship they became aware that they were part of a bigger reality, the body of Christ; this was especially encouraged by the Tanzanians' way of frequently praising God (in the phrase 'Bwana Jesu asifiwe') and praying spontaneously and often through the day. In their company it became easier for their British friends to sense the loving presence and purposes of God and of their constantly inhabiting his Trinitarian community, an ongoing process of spiritual formation. (For a full account of the link see Bill Jones, *Mara!*)

Is it again possible to identify examples of these three qualitatively different stages of growth in the British context, to see how this framework is applicable here? Two examples can be cited, the first being the growth of the Messy Church movement. Bob Jackson in *What Makes Churches Grow?* provides the background to this. His book presents tables and graphs that gather and analyse a range of church data that he has collected over the years. The big message is that statistical evidence since 2000, from a number of dioceses and national surveys, seems to point to a turnaround, and that the Church of England, for example, is now growing, or as Jackson puts it, has more joiners than leavers. This is not about numbers attending Sunday services but the total body of people who attend a wide range of forms of worship during the week as well as on Sundays. Within this, the growth of Messy Church is key. Jackson describes this as the largest church growth phenomenon in Britain in this century so far, and has taken many by surprise as it is not centrally driven but arising locally. For Jackson it is evidence of the Holy Spirit at work 'below the surface' away from national media attention: 'Growing the church is a divine project not a human one' (Jackson 2015, p. 259; see also pp. 150, 171–5).

The Messy Church phenomenon shows churches reaching out to their communities to invite children and parents to craft activities, eating together and celebration and worship. A typical pattern has been for a committed group of leaders and helpers deciding to put on Messy Church. A period of planning and development takes place, with the group advertising the sessions, inviting children and their parents from local schools, providing the craft activities and the food. It is usually labour intensive and sometimes has been hard to sustain for this reason.

This shows how at this stage it is a good example of the first stage of community relationships, that of donors and recipients, in which the children and their parents receive what is being provided for them: all they have to do is turn up. But as Messy Church becomes established and parents become used to what happens they begin to assist with the activities and with providing food. A sense of partnership develops, relieving the pressure on the initial group of leaders and helpers and showing how there is growth into the second stage of community relationships, to partnership between church and community.

In some cases the act of celebration develops into a communion service, though this is quite rare (in one piece of research by George Lings the figure is put at 12 per cent: see Potter and Mobsby 2017, p. 105). But when it does happen it can be powerful, strengthening relationships within the fellowship. As Lucy Moore, one of the founders and leaders of the movement, writes, a well-filled table 'creates community, it fosters belonging, it shouts out silently, "You matter! You are worth it! You are one of us! We are together!"' (Potter and Mobsby 2017, p. 103). Furthermore, communion in the context of a meal can bring everyone together 'by looking at a person who is above and beyond and yet within their own circle', and it 'can be a time of looking outwards to feel a connection with other churches' (p. 107). Above all, it is about helping people 'encounter the holiness of a God beyond our human understanding through the hospitable Christ who welcomes all who are hungry and thirsty, whatever their age, to the table of the King' (p. 110). This all shows that a transition has been made, to the third stage of growth, to the Trinitarian form of community relationships.

The second example comes from the growth of social action projects by churches. When churches develop community projects, such as foodbanks, homeless charities, debt advice centres and drop-in centres, as described earlier (and see also Spencer 2016), it shows the building of trust with a range of partners in the wider community: these projects would not be possible without such growth in the quality of relationships. This in turn shows that they have moved into the second stage – a partnership of equals with neighbours – by listening to people's needs, setting up projects that respond in human and practical ways to those needs, and sometimes entering into formal partnerships with other agencies to achieve those aims. This is highlighted in Nick Spencer's report *Doing Good*; he writes that many of these initiatives are

marked by an emphasis on relationality (people could not thrive outside of caring and secure relationships), hospitality (constantly emphasizing the welcome of the other in community buildings, in church services or relationships), hopefulness and incarnation (offering an ongoing presence in communities spanning generations, even when circumstances were not auspicious). (Spencer 2016, pp. 52–3)

Spencer cites the work of Sanctus St Mark's in Stoke on Trent as an example of this: it supports asylum seekers and refugees as 'a reflection of the self-giving love of Jesus Christ [with a welcome that] aims to be open, non-judgmental and generous, treating all people with equality and dignity, regardless of their economic or social circumstances' (p. 53).

The report makes the following comment on this and other projects it has cited: 'All of these in their own way reflect and embody deep theological commitments and values in their activities, demonstrating authentically Christian ways of "Doing Good"' (p. 53). More than this, they are 'a simultaneous expression of love of God and of neighbour, a way of worshipping God through finding and serving him in others' (p. 13). Drawing on Paul's use of the word 'leitourgia' in 2 Corinthians 9.12, where he uses it to describe what the Corinthians did to supply the needs of others, the report coins the phrase 'social liturgy' to capture the Godly nature of these community projects. Spencer argues that they are examples of social liturgy, of Christians expressing the love that is at the heart of the divine life of God itself (p. 49).

Movement into the third stage becomes possible when this divine love is openly acknowledged, invoked and responded to by all parties. The divine love and action of the Holy Spirit is there all along but the third stage is reached when it is consciously acknowledged and the parties enter into a three-way relationship between church, community and God. At this point, as a church engages in different community projects, it will have not only reached out to members of the wider community in relationships of partnership, it will have consciously inhabited the divine love of the Trinity, which connects them all and can connect them in new and creative ways.

Evangelistic Communication

The case study has illustrated the leading role of evangelism, and how it has taken place in a number of ways. In this section the aim is to identify the different qualitative stages of communication within those ways.

The first stage is expressed in the initial encounter between villagers and the evangelism team. In the narratives this was described as happening through village meetings, when the team would set up a stage area in a public space and the church choir would sing gospel songs with dance, using a PA system to broadcast the music and words as widely as possible. The pastor or guest preacher would then preach, setting out the gospel message in an accessible and compelling way, using the PA system to attract passers-by to come and listen and ask to find out more from a member of the team. In many ways this all demonstrates a simple approach to communication: it is essentially a 'one-way street' in which all the content of the communication is passing from one side to the other. There is no interaction apart from the preacher having earlier listened to the villagers to find the best language and idioms with which to communicate the gospel. It can be described as uni-vocal communication because it does not involve the listener in dialogue with the speaker: the listener will simply receive what is being taught or else walk away with no connectivity. This is not to belittle this form of communication as there are many situations where it is appropriate, and for the purposes of evangelism in Mara it has been proven to be an effective way of making initial contact with villagers.

Akiri adds:

Indeed, this form of communication is justified and necessary because by nature, and as with all preaching sessions, whether indoor or outdoor, or any verbal proclamation, the listeners would not be expected to ask questions. Indeed, open-air verbal proclamation is not the same as being in a seminar or conference room.

A qualitatively different form of communication takes place when an enquirer approaches one of the team and begins to talk. This opens the way to dialogue, to questions and answers, which can respond to the precise concerns and needs of the enquirer much more effectively than public preaching. As we have seen, this happens especially through home visits, when two members of the team spend time with the enquirer responding sensitively and appropriately to their questions while at the same time setting out the content and challenges of the gospel message. This second stage of communication is much more of a two-way street, in which the traffic of the conversation is going in both directions, and was labelled an interactive form of evangelism. It is based on respecting and valuing the enquirer, demonstrated by giving them 'the time of day'.

But the evangelism did not stop there. In Mara evangelism there comes a point where the communication goes beyond the congregation and those who are evangelizing them. This is when the congregation acquires a sense of calling and responsibility for what lies beyond it, for the life of the local community and for spreading the Christian faith to neighbouring villages and communities. It was seen in the way that some of the new churches reached a point where they despatched members of their congregation to a neighbouring village to tell the people there about the Christian faith, becoming proactive in evangelism. In this they made a transition from a dialogue form of communication to a trialogue; they started to engage with a third party – the people in the new village – with all the challenges faced by someone who has been a learner and now becomes a teacher. They must rethink and re-express what they have gained from their own evangelization, so that they can communicate it effectively to the third party. This can be quite a challenge, as any new teacher will testify, but it can also be the most effective way of really grasping and owning the Christian faith; as teachers testify, the most effective way of learning a subject is by teaching it.

But communication can become three-way at a deeper level as well. Sometimes the gospel message finds what the director of evangelism called an 'entry point' into the lives of the villagers. The gospel message connects with their own outlook and beliefs in a deep way, as happened for some when they saw the crucifixion scene in the Jesus film. This can be described as a point of incarnation, of the gospel coming to dwell within the lives and culture of those people. It cannot be easily predicted, or taken for granted, and so is a gift, a moment of grace in which God takes the initiative. The mission team prays for and hopes that this will happen but ultimately it is an interchange that takes place within the hearts of the new Christians, something between them and God himself, who becomes the third party in the communication.

A similar kind of growth can be seen in the companionship link between Wakefield (now Leeds) Diocese and dioceses in Mara region. To begin with, the traffic was mainly in one direction, but quite quickly a partnership was created under the banner of 'bega kwa bega' – standing shoulder to shoulder. In terms of communication this meant listening as well as speaking, learning as well as teaching. This especially happened through visits of representatives from Wakefield to Mara and Mara to Wakefield. Both sets of people travelled to the other side of the world to be informed and educated in a whole host of ways. In conversation, as dialogue partners, they grew in their communication with each other. For the British visitors to Mara this sometimes made a deep impact. They would describe how after their visit the preoccupations of British consumer society would pale into insignificance compared to the challenges of living with poverty in Tanzania, and furthermore, how within the context of that poverty the spiritual life and vitality of the church in Mara would transform their own outlook and values. It was common to hear visitors returning to the UK describe how their priorities in life had been turned upside down and how they now grasped the simple and profound realities of the gospel in a way they had never done before. This showed a kind of conversion taking place, a reverse form of mission in which those who had been donors and educators were now recipients of a spiritual awakening, and those who had been recipients were now evangelizing their British friends, becoming apostles in Christian mission. Here was not only dialogue but God working deeply within the hearts and minds of the visitors: a three-way communication.

The third stage of communication takes place when visitors return home and start to tell others about their experiences. This is a challenge because it can be very hard to convey what has been learnt, and the impact it has made, to those who have not experienced the visit. It means finding the best ways of catching and holding the attention of others, approaching the subject from their point of view and showing how it speaks into their needs and concerns, to allow the conveying of insights and wisdom. The dialogue that took place during the visit now becomes a three-way conversation, or a trialogue, as the point of view of those at home helps to form the communication that takes place, alongside the outlook of the visitors themselves and what they have learnt from their hosts in Mara.

Moving again to an entirely British context, is it possible to identify examples of these three stages of growth in evangelistic communication, to see how this framework can interpret what is happening here?

It is possible to identify at least two of the stages, with growth from one to the other, in church life in the 1990s. In what was termed the Decade of Evangelism, many churches moved away from the traditional 'mission week' style of evangelism, centred around a series of public sermons by an invited evangelist combined with extensive leafleting to invite the community to come and listen and hopefully commit to faith. This was a largely uni-vocal approach to evangelism, in which the preacher did all the speaking and the role of the audience was to listen. This approach was abandoned in favour of the 'nurture group' style of evangelism, represented by courses such as Alpha, Believe, Christianity Explained, Emmaus, Simply Christianity, Start and others. The setting for these was not usually a large church hall but a home or small meeting room in which a group could get to know each other over a meal, then listen to a short talk on an aspect of the Christian faith (with around ten meetings scheduled to cover the whole subject); then there would be a significant amount of time for discussion, with all questions welcomed and no sense of the leader telling participants what they ought to think or believe. This was clearly a major shift in the style of communication and, according to the framework presented here, demonstrated growth from the uni-vocal stage to the interactive dialogue stage. The huge popularity of Alpha and other courses in the years since then has shown that it has been a very fruitful form of growth for churches both in Britain and in many other parts of the world. With declining knowledge of Christianity in society at large, much more dialogue is needed to establish where hearers are coming from and answer questions before people are prepared to make a commitment, and these courses have provided that opportunity, building a sense of community and trust where none existed before.

The question naturally arises about whether there has been further growth, to the three-way form of communication. There is evidence that some churches have invested time and energy in developing their own nurture group courses, specially written and geared towards their local contexts. These have had to take account of the outlook and concerns of the people they are written for, allowing these to form the presentation and content, alongside the original course material from Alpha or elsewhere on the one hand, and on the other the outlook and convictions of those writing them. Three parties, then, have been involved in the process of communicating the gospel, which makes it qualitatively different from the packaged courses. Some commentators believe that these grassroots courses can be the best of all. Mike Booker and Mark Ireland, for example, have written that 'home-grown courses are sometimes even more effective than those taken "off the shelf"' (Booker and Ireland 2003, p. 56)

Three-way communication has possibly gained greater traction in the 'fresh expressions' movement. The process of forming a 'fresh expression' was recently conceptualized by the UK's Fresh Expressions team. Michael Moynagh, reporting on behalf of the team after a wide-ranging survey of fresh expressions 'in consultation with others, not least members of the Church Army's Sheffield [Research] Centre', writes:

Time and again we saw founders of new ecclesial communities being led by the Spirit to listen to their contexts, find simple ways to love and serve people, build community with them, provide opportunities for people to explore following Jesus, encourage tastes of church among those coming to faith and then occasionally 'do it again' – repeat the process in a manner appropriate to the new setting. (Moynagh 2017, p. 44)

However, he adds: 'In practice, the process was seldom so neat. The stages nearly always overlapped, quite often they piled on top of each other and sometimes they were taken in a different order. Typically they rested on a carpet of prayer' (Moynagh 2017, p. 44). Nevertheless, this is a clear and impressive recognition of the need to be contextual. Compared to earlier approaches, such as using special worship services to attract new people to Christian faith, in this approach 'more time is spent "listening" to the context and building relationships before inviting people to come to some sort of event'. In his diagrammatic representation of this, in which the stages of creating a fresh expression are laid out along a horizontal line, the 'listening' stage comes right at the start (p. 45).

Does this, though, represent a genuinely three-way process of communication? The element of evangelism is downplayed in Moynagh's presentation: compared to earlier approaches, he describes the launching of fresh expressions as 'less evangelistically overt' (Moynagh 2017, p. 44). He writes: 'Instead of a narrow focus on evangelism, as in [earlier] approaches, other aspects of the kingdom come more explicitly into play, notably "loving and serving" (works of mercy or justice) and "building community". These do not arise after evangelism' (p. 45). The question is whether the downplaying of evangelism results in the muffling of one of the three voices in the three-way communication. The context clearly has its voice through this strong emphasis on 'listening' to its people, and the Christians seeking to serve its people have their voice; but what of the gospel itself in its fullness and challenge, as exemplified in Mara's approach to evangelism? There is a question here about Moynagh's approach as a whole, which will need to be discussed when comparing all the approaches (see Chapter 4). But for now, the immediate point is that all this shows how the voice of those receiving the Christian faith is now being well recognized in current thinking, opening the possibility for three-way communication.

Sacramental Expression

What does the case study reveal about the stages of growth of sacramental expression in the life of the church?

In their description of village evangelism the new Christians and the pastor described how the choir, with its lively singing and dancing, played an important part in winning over the villagers. Drawing on a first-millennium understanding of sacraments that included a wide range of Christian experiences that were 'hinting symbols or types in which the old order is seen as an anticipation of the new' (see above, p. 21), this showed a form of sacramental expression of the faith, bringing a foretaste of the reality of God's salvation into bodily expression in singing and dance, as important as verbal communication for some. Here was a spontaneous and informal sacramentality that touched the hearts and lives of those watching, listening and joining in.

A second stage of sacramentality is also apparent in the case study. After preparation by the local priest, the members of a new church are brought to baptism by the local priest, to confirmation by a bishop and then to regular Holy Communion. This is different from the first stage not only because these are officially designated as sacraments of the church but because those administering and receiving them have an intentionality about them. In the first stage the singing and dance were rehearsed but the sacramentality was not planned by the participants. It would just happen on the basis of the spiritual receptivity of those watching and listening, and ultimately on whether God chose to reveal himself within them. The performers would concentrate on producing a committed performance, and leave God to do the rest. The first stage of sacramentality, then, can be described as spontaneous and irregular, coming from God as and when he chooses. In the second stage, expressed through the formal sacraments, those administering and receiving the sacraments play an instrumental part in what takes place, by recalling Jesus' words, pouring water, laying hands on heads, breaking and eating bread and drinking wine.

On the basis of scripture and in particular on Jesus' commands in the Gospels to be baptized and to repeat his actions at the Last Supper in memory of him, they know that God will also play his part in making the signs efficacious. As the Catechism of the Book of Common Prayer puts it, they are 'given unto us, ordained by Christ himself'. But this requires a level of belief and commitment on the part of those receiving them: they have to believe that God exists, that Jesus Christ is his Son, that Jesus issued these commands as recorded in the Gospels, that they are binding on his followers and that when they do them God brings into effect the grace of his presence within them. Hence this second stage of sacramentality is 'intentional' in that both human and divine participants intend the sacrament to take place.

A third stage can also be detected. It is hinted at in the words of one of the ordinands in his description of why some villagers are attracted towards becoming a Christian:

> when they see church people visit and care for people in the community abandoned by their families, going to their homes, praying with them, sharing the word of God and showing that even though they have been abandoned they are part of God's family, the onlookers have said that these Christians are 'the true church'.

This statement is revealing because it makes a link between the whole life of a church – its community service as well as its worship and fellowship – with some kind of divine presence signified by the phrase 'the true church'. Somehow this local church is embodying a qualitative difference from other churches, a kind of 'anticipation of the new'. It shows how a church might begin to fulfil the high vocation that Henri de Lubac gave the church, drawn on by Dulles: 'If Christ is the sacrament of God, the Church is for us the sacrament of Christ; she represents him, in the full and ancient meaning of the term, she really makes him present. She not only carries on his work, but she is his very continuation ...' (see above, p. 45).

And as 'an anticipation of the new' she is a sacrament of the kingdom. As we have seen, Dulles points out:

By its visible presence the Church reminds men [and women] of God's Kingdom and keeps alive their hope for the blessings of eternal life. But it is more than a sign. It betokens the actual presence, in a hidden way, of that to which it points. What is essential to the Kingdom, the reconciling grace of Christ, is truly at work in the Church, although not exclusively in the Church. The Church, with the help of the gospel and of the Holy Spirit, is able to discern and celebrate the gifts of God to men [and women].

The church's official sacraments still have a role, one of clarifying this: 'It assembles in manifest visibility about the altar of the Lord and proclaims the Lord's death until he comes. At the Eucharist the Church becomes more than ever a sacramental sign of the heavenly Jerusalem' (Dulles 1987, p. 114).

The life of the church as a whole, then, both assembly for worship and dispersal for mission, fellowship and community service, personal discipleship and institutional ordering, can be seen as a sacrament of Christ, as Christ is a sacrament of God. This third stage of sacramentality, which is sometimes recognized in a local church when others see it as being genuinely Christ-like, a fruit of a sacrificial maturity, can therefore be described as a holistic stage, because it encompasses its whole life. It cannot, though, be taken for granted. When others start to see division and selfishness in congregational life they will very quickly stop seeing it as 'the true church'.

Moving to the British context, is it possible to identify examples of these three stages of growth in sacramentality, to see how this framework reads and interprets what is happening here?

For the first stage, that of spontaneous and informal sacramentality, it is necessary to look more widely than the church's practice of the official sacraments. In *Doorways to the Sacred* (2017) a range of leaders in the Fresh Expressions of Church movement describe its developing and increasingly rich sacramental life. It is testimony to a growing appreciation of sacramentality in the movement. John Drane writes on 'the glory of God in everyday life' and provides a good example of this. He recalls Augustine of Hippo who listed more than 300 things that he regarded as sacraments, 'and while they included distinctively ecclesiastical rituals such as baptism, Eucharist, penance and chrism, he also listed things like contemplation, bowing one's head, taking off one's shoes, music and singing, along with reconciliation and other social actions as authentic expressions of divine realities' (Potter and Mobsby 2017, p. 25). In this vein, Drane quotes the spiritual experiences of young snowboarders and skaters, as well as many musicians and artists who have described moments of absorption in their work in which there is a 'connection to some ultimate reality'. While he does not actually describe these as sacraments, Drane comments that there 'are significant missional connections to be made with historic understandings of the sacramental, though in order to make them we will need an expansive understanding of the *missio Dei* and a more radical understanding of the nature of sacrament' (p. 21).

In another essay in the book, Olive Fleming Drane outlines a way of identifying sacraments within a range of spiritual experiences. She describes, for example, a training course for social workers, in which 'the sharing of bread and melted ice water/wine made a natural sacramental connection for those who were familiar with the biblical narrative, and it potentially became so for others [when] those who knew the story shared it with them'. The combination of an action with a well-known narrative, then, generates the sacramentality. She argues that the narrative of story 'is the thing that denotes otherwise ordinary experiences as vehicles of divine grace'. But such stories need not just be from the Bible. Drane wonders if 'the story of our lives' should also inform 'a broader understanding of sacrament as a transformational experience of God-in-Christ' (Potter and Mobsby 2017, p. 38). She also appeals to Augustine for validation of this broader and inclusive understanding of sacraments. Her essay, and the others in the same volume, show a new openness to first-stage sacramentality in the growth of churches in the British context.

For examples of the second stage of sacramentality, which highlights the place of the official sacraments in church growth, the book does not ignore the challenges. Jonathan Clark points out that for those involved in church growth 'very few see the sacraments themselves as an integral part of their sharing in the mission of God to the world'. But he argues for the need to counter this: 'if the sacraments are gifts of God by which we share in God's grace, they are key sites of God's presence in the world. They are places where the miracle of God's breaking into human lives is again and again repeated' (Potter and Mobsby 2017, p. 66). Clark's essay makes a strong case for making them more accessible, such as having an 'open font', linking baptism with preaching the gospel, so that as people respond to God's word in their hearts they can respond by being baptized there and then.

A different example of the sacraments finding a place in fresh expressions is from the Messy Church movement, this time with respect to communion. While, as mentioned above, only around 12 per cent of Messy Churches include a communion service within their sessions, this is likely to increase. In her contribution to *Doorways to the Sacred*, Lucy Moore, a founder and leader of the movement, argues that communion is 'a means Jesus provided for anyone to taste and see that God is good, to experience for themselves the intimacy of relationship that comes through eating and drinking together, the reality of the bread and wine echoing the reality of God's unconditional love'. This leads her to argue passionately that:

> we should probably try to have it more often, so that it becomes yet another means for anyone to encounter the love of God and for God to act in ways beyond our control. It won't amaze you to know that I am more and more convinced that Communion is a mystery that Jesus has provided to help anyone come closer to him, including people

with disabilities, people with different academic abilities, of different ages and levels of damage in their life experience, those nearer or closer to God. The more I learn from Christ in the stranger and the more I see him in people who have never been part of organized religion before, the more convinced I am that we are all so many gazillion miles away from understanding and appreciating what Communion really means that, as a Church, we should arguably simply make it available to everyone Jesus is drawing closer to him. (Potter and Mobsby 2017, p. 104)

In other words, watch this space for an increase in those Messy Churches moving to the second stage of sacramentality, a stage in which there will be fewer barriers, and even an open table, to encourage enquirers to take communion.

Some of the authors in *Doorways to the Sacred* also move towards the notion of the church in all aspects of its life being recognized as sacramental – being a sacrament of Christ as a whole – the third stage of sacramentality within church growth. Adrian Chatfield provides one example:

We might say that Christ is the great sacrament, and that all our sacramental acts are performed as if Christ himself were doing them. That is what the doctrine of the real presence of Christ in the Holy Eucharist really means. It means too that the Church, as the body of Christ here on earth continuing to do 'these works and greater than these', acts *in loco Christi* through the sacraments. When we act, heaven breaks in, the kingdom comes a little closer, and the promise of *shalom* becomes real in one more person's life. (Potter and Mobsby 2017, pp. 152–3)

It is hard at the moment to find examples of fresh expressions promoting this third stage of sacramentality but the fact that some of its leaders are encouraging it in this direction is significant. It shows the germ of this kind of development and also points to the relevance of the interpretative framework developed at the start of this section.

Community Service

What does the Tanzanian case study reveal about stages of growth in a church's service of its community?

At the beginning, as churches were being formed in villages, they were essentially friendship groups, which meant they lacked organizational structure and the ability to make formal decisions. They were not able to set up and run community projects, such as a nursery. However, the villagers themselves would still look out for and help their neighbours, as and when needs arose. Evidence of this was provided by one of the ordinands when he described how the mutual support of the Anglican congregation, a support that had attracted new members, was seen especially in the way members helped those in need. Here was a case of actions speaking louder than words, as reported by an ordinand who said that 'the members of the church are well respected in the community'. Community service, then, could be described as spontaneous and informal.

As the church became more established, with elected elders and a simple constitution adopted from the diocese, and support from a nearby priest, with the official sacraments now playing a part in their common life, the church could decide to take on a community project of some kind. With village churches this would usually be on a small scale, one of the most common forms reported in interviews being a nursery that would meet on weekdays for infants. This might meet under a tree in the drier times of the year, but if the church had its own building this would obviously be a much better location. The parents would pay a small contribution for the teacher but the congregation would provide validation and oversight of the school. This second kind of service can be described as 'singular' because it is all about providing a single piece of community support which has a simple, clear and agreed aim and well-defined objectives to achieve it.

This hints at what a third stage of community service might be. When a church is well established, being recognized by others as holding its own and being one of the corporate members of the village community, it has the opportunity to become a hub of several services, or a multiple service provider. This will usually happen through the church setting up partnerships with other organizations for support and funding. In Mara this would usually be through the diocese which has been keen to find opportunities to establish a range of development, health and educational initiatives. The diocese has been good at securing funding from international donors because of these partnerships with village churches and communities, with one leading to the other. So now, in Mara region, a number of parish churches host a range of community services, from dispensaries to orphan support to vocational training centres to education by extension centres, as well as nurseries. Furthermore, a few churches have become the hosts for hand-pumped wells and rainwater harvest systems to collect fresh water. These are an especially powerful sign of the church doing all it can to serve those who are not its members, because what could be more basic and life-giving than the gift of clean water? When a church achieves this stage of community service it can therefore be described as a community hub providing multiple services.

When churches have achieved this third stage they can then make an impact in other ways. In the interviews we heard how the diocese's commitment to various kinds of development projects, education at various levels and health care had prepared the ground for evangelism. There were reports of farmers who had attended farming enrichment courses at the local Anglican farm development centres in Mara region who then wanted to become Anglicans. The same was true of villagers in Serengeti district who came across the church's safe house and its campaigning work against FGM, and who were then attracted to the church. But, as mentioned, all these projects were pursued for their own sake and not for an ulterior evangelistic motive. The benefits for evangelism were a by-product.

These three stages of growth can quite easily be identified in church life in Britain. As far as the first stage is concerned, Moynagh's research into fresh expressions of church has demonstrated an intimate connection between these often informal groups starting up and their 'loving and serving' those in need they come across, supporting each to face a specific need in their context. Building community and exploring discipleship then tends to follow on from this initial service (Moynagh 2017, pp. 44–7). He goes on to advocate this kind of 'serving first journey' as the archetypal way in which churches start and grow, a view that will be evaluated in the next chapter. Here it is simply necessary to note the increasingly important place that community service takes in the growth of the church, a correspondence with Mara's growth model.

As far as the second and third stages are concerned, we have already seen how many churches across all denominations now have community projects (see above, pp. 53–4). Some of these are in the second or 'singular' stage with just one project, while many others are in the third or 'multiple hub' stage with several projects on the go, their buildings and congregations becoming centres for a range of initiatives that serve the local population in a varied set of ways. There is evidence that the size and impact of these projects has been increasing even while Sunday church attendance has been declining. Nick Spencer in the report *Doing Good* refers to some research done in 2014 on the impact of local churches in deprived communities in England. A survey was conducted asking people whether they had accessed community (non-statutory) services in the last 12 months, and if so whether these had been provided by churches or church groups. Around half (48 per cent) of adults had accessed community services, with around half of these (51 per cent) accessing services provided by churches or church groups. Using the Office of National Statistics population figures for England, 'this equated to just over 10 million adults using church "services", using the word explicitly to exclude the traditionally "religious" services of Sunday, Christmas, Easter and Harvest services, and baptisms, weddings and funerals' (Spencer 2016, p. 45). Spencer unpacks these impressive figures in the following way:

The services listed included foodbanks, community events (e.g. lunch clubs or cafes), healthy living activities (e.g. community nursing, exercise classes, healthy eating courses), relationship support, financial education and advice, access to computers/the internet, and providing opportunities for volunteering. The most frequently used community services were children and youth services, cultural events, and activities for older people, but churches also provided support for asylum seekers, for people with addictions, counselling and 'street pastoring'. In other words, the level of community activity among the churches was huge. (Spencer 2016, p. 45)

The growth of this community service is one of the most notable features of church life in contemporary Britain. Furthermore, Samuel Wells, Russell Rook and David Barclay have suggested, in their book *For Good*, that churches now have a key role of cultivating key social goods, not just eradicating evils, for the community as a whole. Up to now many have thought social action was to play a part, alongside the state, in eradicating 'the evils of want, idleness, ignorance, disease and squalor', to use the language of the Beveridge Report of 1942 which laid the foundations of the post-war welfare state. But in an era when the limitations of what the state can or is willing to do become ever clearer, it is up to the church to be much more proactive in building a good and healthy society. Now, more than 75 years after the Beveridge Report, the authors propose that church social action should especially concentrate on cultivating five common goods, which they name as 'relationship, creativity, partnership, compassion and joy'. While the church should still hold the state accountable for addressing the five great evils, it should not confuse this with advancing these goods, which the state is in no position to do. Churches, locally and nationally, need to work actively and tirelessly to model and cultivate these goods, especially through creating cross-generational community and in cherishing people for what they are, not what they are not (Wells *et al.* 2017, p. 12).

There will long, perhaps always, be a role for the state in alleviating the deficits of society. But the church is invariably better placed than the state to cultivate society's assets – its social goods that can be apparent in adversity as much as comfort, and as absent in places of splendour as much as of squalor. Reflection on the Beveridge Report 75 years after its publication offers the churches a moment to identify those goods, to examine closely how its activities are uniquely suited to advance them, and to refine its practice so as to make itself better at doing so. In the process, the churches may well enhance society: but they will undoubtedly renew themselves. (Wells *et al.* 2017, pp. 17–18)

In these kinds of terms, then, becoming a community hub – the third stage of community service identified in the interpretative framework of this chapter – is not just about addressing certain social needs through a number of community projects; it is about inhabiting a very positive role in the community at large, of generating those five great goods. It is, in short, to become a hub *for* social good, without being seen to take over what should arguably be the role of the state, or being co-opted into the state's agenda.

Discipleship

In Mara region, what was the pathway that villagers followed as they encountered the Christian faith through evangelism and church life? As elsewhere, the focus of this section is on the social nature of church growth, the community profile of what is happening, rather than on the internal or psychological nature of discipleship. For the sake of consistency with earlier sections three key stages of discipleship will be identified: the initial stage, an intermediate stage and then the final stage of mature faith.

Evangelism in Mara began with public preaching and singing and dance, a shop window for newcomers to come and see what Christianity is all about. The pastor described how he and his helpers would have conversations with anyone who expressed an interest in finding out more. Then, if they wanted to learn more, he and another would arrange to visit their home so that a longer and more reflective conversation could take place. The pastor would present the invitation and the challenge of Christian faith and membership of the church and then give their hosts the freedom to choose whether to take it up.

To have invited the pastor to come to their homes indicates a positive step on the part of the villagers. Yet they had not yet made a deliberate commitment to becoming a Christian. So the type of relationship in this first stage of discipleship could be described as one of enquiry, in which they show interest and want to find out more, but are not yet ready to commit to a longer-term relationship.

A second stage becomes apparent when a group of villagers make such a commitment and form themselves into a community of faith under the guidance and support of a priest. They have repented of their sins and committed to following Christ for the rest of their lives. They have set out on their journey with him, in the company of others, and now they will meet on a regular basis to read the Bible together, to pray and to support each other. They choose their elders to lead and coordinate their common life. The priest will visit to teach them and prepare them first for baptism and later for confirmation. In this intermediate stage the villagers have therefore moved from being enquirers to being like apprentices: they have literally become disciples or learners, on the basis of a definite commitment, to be taught and guided by the practical example of other Christians to learn how to live the way of the Lord.

The next step is confirmation by the bishop, after which they can start to receive Holy Communion (whenever the priest comes to preside at the Eucharist), which they will continue to do on a regular basis. They will also begin to send a regular contribution to the diocese as their 'parish share'. They have crossed a line into full adult membership of the church.

Akiri elaborates:

In many parts of Tanzania, people regard the confirmation service as a significant rite of passage. Parents will spend money on shoes and elegant white dresses for girls and women, and suits for young boys and mature men. In some parts, for example Tarime, the emphasis is more on the communal dimension of the rite. The parish, collectively including the candidates, donates thanksgiving offering to the diocese well in advance of the day of confirmation and raises money for a communal meal. On the day of confirmation, and soon after service, the candidates take photos with the bishop and sit at table to share a meal with him. The rest of the congregation also shares a meal. This signifies both the crossing of the line by the candidates into full adult membership of the church and a sense of belonging in a big family of God.

They are no longer 'apprentices' but have become fully responsible, along with all the other churches of the diocese, for the life of the diocese itself.

As mentioned, they can now be constituted as a parish in their own right and send representatives to diocesan synods for the governing of the diocese. They have become full members of the body of Christ. Their discipleship has entered a third stage, like that of 'friendship' in the sense in which Jesus says to his disciples, 'I do not call you servants any longer, because the servant does not know what the master is doing; but I have called you friends, because I have made known to you everything that I have heard from my Father' (John 15.15). In Mara growth this is the stage when churches begin to take responsibility for the life of the church as a whole through the empowering approach of being 'self-extending, self-supporting and self-governing'.

A similar example of three different stages of growth in community discipleship, of enquiry, apprenticeship and friendship, is found in the Roman Catholic Church's 'Rite of Christian

Initiation of Adults' (RCIA). It describes a first stage as the 'period of evangelization', when enquirers begin to clarify what they are seeking and the questions they are asking, and take on board the gospel message for the first time. During this 'pre-catechumenate' period, teaching is given to people who are interested in learning more about the Catholic faith. The sessions cover basic information and communicate the fundamentals of the faith. 'The church is offering here an invitation to initial conversion. There is no obligation involved in attending these meetings – they are intended to help a person decide whether they want to continue learning about the Faith' (US Bishops, *Guidelines to RCIA*). This corresponds well with the first stage above, also described as one of enquiry.

The second stage is called the 'period of the catechumenate', in which the focus is to learn what it means to follow Christ in his church. This is an extended period during which the candidates are given suitable pastoral formation and guidance, aimed at training them in the Christian life. This is achieved through formal teaching, encouragement to turn to God in prayer, learning how to bear witness to the faith, loving neighbour and learning to work actively with others to spread the gospel. There is no time limit to this stage: it lasts as long as each person needs. When the catechumen is ready they will be baptized. They normally prepare for baptism during Lent and are baptized and admitted to the Eucharist at Easter. This stage clearly corresponds to the apprenticeship stage described above, though in Mara baptism may happen earlier in the process with admittance to communion taking place after confirmation by the bishop.

The third stage is of mature Christian faith, whole-life discipleship and full membership of the church, which lasts for a lifetime. The Church of England report *Setting God's People Free* has taken forward the process of thinking through what this means for discipleship, away from ecclesiastical contexts and into the contexts of contemporary society. The following paragraph provides a good pointer to what it is advocating:

We think that a clear, consistently communicated vision for lay people and their role in society 'Monday to Saturday' will play a vital role in inspiring an emerging generation to discover 'whole-of-life' vocation and calling in ways that lead to confident engagement with the urgent challenges and opportunities of our time – for example, instilling the Christian story across our schools and to young people, repurposing enterprise around the common good, bringing hope to the most marginalized as doctors, lawyers and care-givers, and redeeming local and national politics. (Church of England 2017, 4.1)

Returning to the RCIA process and viewing it as a whole, Bishop Graham Cray, one of the leaders of the fresh expressions movement, comments that 'this Roman Catholic sequence is helpful for churches from other traditions' (in Potter and Mobsby 2017, p. 10). He explains how it correlates with a typical discipleship pattern within fresh expressions:

The first stage may well take place through informal conversation, through hospitality in homes, or discussion events in neutral venues. All are welcome to start attending the regular worship of the fresh expression at any time, but it is not a requirement, and would be a step too far for some people. The second stage could involve an Alpha, Pilgrim or Christianity Explored course, or something specifically created for this group of people. It is more likely to be a group process and should normally include an invitation to attend worship as part of the process of learning, without attendance implying anything more than enquiry. In more liturgical or new monastic fresh expressions entry into the second stage may be marked publicly and liturgically, as in the Roman Catholic process. Both stages can be arranged for children. Fresh expressions like Messy Church could plan them for whole family groups. (Potter and Mobsby 2017, pp. 10–11)

Finally, Cray says, 'Baptism, confirmation or the renewal of baptismal vows makes the public transition from being an enquirer to a disciple, from welcome guest to family member' (Potter and Mobsby 2017, p. 11). Compared to the description above, this shifts the use of the term 'disciple' from the second to the third stage, and within that stage uses the term 'family member' rather than 'friend'. But in other respects it is close to what has been observed in Mara growth and shows, once again, that the stages framework drawn from that context corresponds in many ways with what is happening in discipleship development in Britain and elsewhere at the moment.

This finally completes our survey of the six dimensions of church growth in Mara and in Britain. A comprehensive summary of the findings is presented in the summary table. The question that now requires an answer is whether the resulting framework *as a whole* is a good one for reading and interpreting church growth in Britain and other contexts. In other words, having demonstrated a whole range of points of correspondence and therefore comparability between what is happening there and what is happening in these other contexts, can Mara's model of growth as a whole support and inform what is happening within them?

Summary of the six dimensions of church growth

	First stage of growth	Second stage of growth	Third stage of growth
Organizational growth	Friendship group	Voluntary association	Public utility
Congregational relationships	Donor–recipient	Partnership	Trinitarian
Evangelistic communication	Uni-vocal	Interactive	Three-way
Sacramental expression	Spontaneous	Intentional	Holistic
Community service	Occasional	Singular	Multiple
Discipleship	Enquiry stage	Apprenticeship	Friendship

4

From Theory to Practice

Which Framework?

The underlying purpose of this book is to encourage and inform church growth. It has produced a six-dimensional framework of understanding drawn from a case study of exemplary growth in Tanzania. There is now a need to compare this framework with one or two others in current thinking to assess which might be the best at unlocking the secret of church growth in other contexts such as in Britain.

Church Planting

One of the most influential models in British churches today is that of 'church planting'. A large church will typically send a team of 30 to 50 people to another church that is struggling and might be under threat of closure. With the agreement of the congregation of that church the team will arrive en masse and work to revitalize it. This is done through using lively and engaging worship, with strong preaching and teaching, as a shop window to the surrounding community. Neighbours, colleagues and friends are invited to join, and through presentations, discussions on life issues, Alpha courses or similar, members of the community are encouraged to explore the Christian faith further. If they commit to it they then join a house group that meets near where they live. They also become involved in helping to lead the church's congregational life. Michael Moynagh in *Church in Life* describes the dynamics of this approach: 'The new congregation scales up quickly and rapidly takes financial responsibility for its staff, perhaps adding more. Expanding on a self-sustaining basis, at its best it plants a further congregation' (Moynagh 2017, p. 39). He identifies five stages in this form of 'worship-first' church growth:

1 Preparation.
2 The planting of the team in the struggling church with worship and preaching as its public face.
3 Events and courses to attract new members.
4 Small groups to receive and deepen the involvement of new members.
5 Sending off another team to do the same elsewhere.

A 2016 study of church planting in east London, *Love, Sweat and Tears*, produced by the Centre for Theology and Community, provides a detailed and insightful description of some successful examples of this. The first plant was in St Paul's Shadwell, from Holy Trinity Brompton, with four other plants developing from this one. The attendance figures show that the congregations generally doubled in size, with a sizeable proportion of newcomers being new believers. The report also tells of how these churches saw an explosion in social action as the numerical growth increased the capacity of the churches to host a range of activities, from foodbanks and debt advice to community organizing, sometimes in partnership with schools and mosques, and it tells how the churches are now making substantial payments into the diocesan common fund. The report highlights the centrality of prayer and of keeping God in the centre of the picture:

'Church planting is an art, not a science ... and seeing God in it is important.' God famously moves in a mysterious way. The church planters in this report have often been able to identity how events and processes which seemed unconnected at the time were in fact equipping them for their current journey. (Centre for Theology and Community 2016a, p. 103)

The report also emphasizes the importance of being intentional about church growth, that it needs to be properly planned and patiently worked for: 'For a church to grow and keep growing its leaders need to be thinking about how to prepare for this, encourage it and enable it at every stage of the process' (Centre for Theology and Community 2016a, p. 104). Another report from the Centre for Theology and Community, *Church Growth in East London* (2016), shows how this emphasis on intentionality is key to growth not only for churches in the Evangelical and Charismatic traditions but for those from the Catholic tradition in the same diocese.

How does all this compare with Mara's·model of growth? There are a number of similarities, which include the following.

Both involve careful preparation that includes the respective diocese, and investment of human and financial resources. In Mara region the pastors and the diocesan staff as well as members of the diocesan committees had to set aside time for evangelism and approach it in a strategic way. The costs involved, including accommodation, a PA system, transport and food, together amounted to a sizeable sum of money for such poor dioceses. In London each church plant required considerable planning and a start-up investment of £50,000 from the planting church. In both cases, then, there is a clear institutional dimension of growth involving intentional strategic planning and delivery.

Both approaches give a central role to lively and engaging worship, which becomes a kind of shop window for the life of the church. In Mara there was a sacramental dimension to this. The same can be said to be true of the east London plants where the charismatic style of worship can often host a powerful sense of the presence of God's Spirit among the worshippers.

In both models there is an emphasis on evangelistic teaching, both in worship and in the courses and home visiting that takes place. The combination of a clear and sometimes challenging gospel teaching with an interactive style of communication, which includes being sensitive and responsive to the culture of the context, is present in both.

Both models clearly include growth in service of the wider community, impressively so in the case of the east London church plants, and they also place discipleship development at the centre of their congregational life.

But there is an important contrast between the two models as far as community relationships are concerned. In Mara, while the diocesan evangelism team come from elsewhere, once they have shared the gospel they leave the village, usually after one week. Their approach does not involve the permanent planting of a new group of people in the village community. This means, crucially, that when the new church is launched it is constituted and led *by* local villagers *for* local villagers: it is inherently contextual in a way in which the church plant, made up of a group arriving from elsewhere, is not. The *Love, Sweat and Tears* report gives considerable space to the challenges and issues surrounding integrating the arriving group with the continuing congregation. It is clear that this process was handled well and many new local people came to join the church plants, but it illustrates the challenges and risks involved in this model. In Mara these are avoided (though there are risks in a different way if the new local congregations are not sufficiently supported in the early stages of their life). This contrast shows the church plant model underemphasizing the need for inherent community embeddedness compared to the Mara model, and this may be a contributing factor to why church planting has not spread very widely beyond the cultural world of London and its satellite towns that have hosted it. While it has been fruitful, it has not shown the degree of fruitfulness found in Mara, where church growth has taken place in every part of the region.

If the Mara model could be translated into other contexts then it could prove, on current evidence, to be the most promising of all. Moynagh reports on a range of other limitations to the church planting model which since 2000 have increasingly come to light (Moynagh 2017, pp. 40–1). For example, he reports that accumulating evidence suggests that in the global North 'church-growth influenced plants connect better with lapsed church-goers than those with little or no church background, whose numbers are steadily growing' (p. 41). While church planting has a place, then, especially from large churches that have the capacity to give away a group of their own people to areas where they can connect with a local population, it is not going to produce the kind of self-replicating growth that is desperately needed.

Fresh Expressions

The fresh expressions movement, on the other hand, has community embeddedness at the heart of its growth. It is the approach that Moynagh extensively advocates in his books; *Church in Life* is based on his study of the movement. One problem is that fresh expressions come in all shapes and sizes and it is not possible to describe a typical example, but in 2012 he published a concise and helpful definition, reiterated in *Church in Life*. He defines fresh expressions to be:

> *Missional* – through the Spirit, they are birthed by Christians mainly among people who do not normally attend church.
> *Contextual* – they seek to serve their context and fit the circumstances of the people in it.
> *Formational* – their leaders aim to make disciples.
> *Ecclesial* – their leaders intend them not to be stepping stones to an existing church, but to become church for the people they reach. The community may be a new congregation of a local church or, if it is not part of a local church, a church in its own right. (Moynagh 2017, p. 3)

There are some important connections between this list and the dimensions of church growth identified in Mara. In each case the growth is among people who do not normally attend church, so they are both 'missional' in Moynagh's use of that term. The congregations in each place serve their contexts by meeting human needs in various ways. Growth in discipleship, in following the way of Jesus, is integral to church growth.

And, in contrast to the church planting model, in both cases new congregations are formed *by* and *for* the people who join them, so fitting the circumstances of those people (in Mara's case within rural village life), so are inherently and impressively contextual. In Mara this is demonstrated by their electing their own elders even while being supported by a distant parish and diocese.

However, there are some important differences. One concerns the way outsiders interact with the community. In the case of fresh expressions they are described as 'founders' or a 'founding team' (Moynagh 2017, p. 44) who listen, love, serve and build. It may be two, three or a dozen mature Christians who arrive from outside and embed themselves into the local community, becoming part of its everyday life. They will take time listening to that community and finding out its needs, then 'loving and serving' those people in whatever ways are appropriate. They may well organize community events that can help to launch a congregation. 'The journey begins with the world, with all its passions and needs. Founders pay attention to these and discern which they are called to address' (p. 46). Through this they build community 'as people form relationships in the context of a "loving and serving" initiative'. This can take different forms, and within this process members of the community can explore discipleship and slowly be led to faith. Moynagh describes some distinct pathways to faith, which can take years, helped along by 'signposts to Jesus' (pp. 48–50).

Clearly there is a big contrast here with the Mara model, to do with the timescale and manner in which the outsiders interact with the locals. In Mara's case the input by the outsiders takes place right at the start in an intensive week of public meetings and home visiting. There is an immediacy and concentration about their contact with the villagers, making a clear and definite offer and invitation that asks for an immediate response. At the end of the week they leave. With fresh expressions it is longer term, much less focused, and open-ended. Whether the Mara approach can work in different contexts is considered below. But this contrast highlights the fact that

Moynagh does not include certain dimensions of growth that we found to be central in Mara, and were validated in Avery Dulles' summary of recent ecclesiology (Chapter 2). In particular, two dimensions are missing: the evangelistic and the sacramental.

In Mara we saw how an interactive evangelism was at the heart of the whole endeavour, an evangelism rooted in strong congregational relationships and drawing from an inherited legacy dating back to the nineteenth-century European missionary movement when evangelism and service of the community were at the heart of the work of missionary societies.

But it seems to be a low priority in *Church in Life*, as previously noted in the discussion on evangelistic communication (see above, pp. 75–6). A question was raised there about the UK Fresh Expressions team's approach as a whole, which downplayed evangelism compared to earlier forms of mission. In its place Moynagh advocates a 'less evangelistically overt' approach (Moynagh 2017, p. 44), which avoids 'a narrow focus on evangelism' (p. 45), and is later described as 'companionship as mission', in which the mature Christian leads the enquirer to faith by standing side by side with them in friendship (pp. 392–3). This is a very attractive proposition, but does it allow definite teaching of the Christian faith to take place and does it enable the difficult challenges of the gospel to be presented, as happened in Mara with opposition to FGM? Put another way, does it give proper expression to the calling of the church to be a 'herald', as in Dulles' ecclesiology? Evangelism receives only two brief references in the index of *Church in Life*, and the implication is that it is not a priority for fresh expressions. If this is actually the case, and given that Moynagh describes many of the fresh expressions communities as short-lived, is there perhaps a deficiency here, one that Mara's model of growth corrects?

The sacramental dimension of church life, furthermore, is almost absent from his discussion. This is not to say that fresh expressions of church do not have sacramental elements: as we have seen, in many places they are increasingly present (see Potter and Mobsby, *Doorways to the Sacred*). What this suggests is that Moynagh's conceptualization of church growth, at least in *Church in Life*, is missing a second important dimension of growth, that of sacramental expression, which becomes even clearer when it is compared with Dulles' ecclesiological overview.

The Mara model of growth, then, with its six interconnected dimensions, picks up more aspects of ecclesiology as well as more elements of contemporary church practice than two of the other leading contenders. In Chapter 3 of this book we saw how each of the elements of practice is present (to some extent) in Britain and especially within growing churches in this context. But the challenge is that these elements are not present together in the way they are in Mara. It is the package as a whole that is yet to find clear expression in the British context. So let us now explore how it might be embraced here, especially in ordinary, medium-sized churches, by first distilling some initial practical principles of the approach, shorn of their cultural clothing from the Tanzanian context, and then seeing how they might be expressed here.

Some Practical Principles

The Mara approach to growth, as we have seen, is rooted in community service, led by an interactive evangelism that includes sacramental expression, with deeply respectful congregational relationships, and bearing fruit in discipleship and institutional enlargement. Unlike the other approaches, it embodies all six ecclesiological dimensions of Catholic church life identified by Dulles (see Chapter 2 above). The question is whether this combination of elements, with a prominent role for evangelism, can be expressed in British and other contexts. What practical steps are needed and, in particular, how can evangelism can be given such a prominent place in this way especially when we recall the wariness with which many Western people respond to anything that suggests proselytism?

The fresh expressions movement, as described by Moynagh, seems to avoid evangelism; it has gradually de-emphasized evangelism in favour of companionship as mission. This has been in response to earlier approaches to evangelism, such as in church planting, which have not led to the breakthrough wanted by so many. Can the Mara model, with its distinctive combination of contextually embedded churches launched through planned and concentrated evangelism, have something different and invigorating to offer mission here?

To answer this question some further clarification is needed about the initial practical principles of Mara growth. To begin with, it became clear from the interviews that growth occurred on the back of community service, which established trust between the wider community and the church. This service took place in a whole variety of ways, responding to specific needs in different contexts, and was undertaken for its own sake as part of the holistic mission of the church, rather than with an ulterior evangelistic motive, but it had the effect of building bridges with the people of the area. As with fresh expressions, in Moynagh's presentation (see above, pp. 75–6), it is a presupposition of the other dimensions of growth. The first practical principle is therefore simple yet profound in its scope: *before anything else, the church needs to be actively engaged in serving its community in a contextually appropriate and committed way.*

A key step was then taken when the leadership of the churches, whether at parish or diocesan level, decided that a deliberate initiative would be taken to communicate the gospel to new people, invite them to accept its grace and form their own church, in a structured and contextually respectful way. This was not a decision to seek institutional growth as such but was a decision *for* evangelism. Nor was it a decision to be oblique, following Bob Jackson's principle of obliquity (Jackson 2015, p. 75), in which it seems that one thing is being sought while the real goal is something else, in this case bringing people to faith. Instead the clear intention and aim was simply and radically to offer the precious gift of the gospel to those who did not yet have it, honouring and respecting their decision to accept or not accept it. So a second principle needs to be about making this kind of evangelism central to church life.

In one respect making evangelism a priority is unsurprising. Many churches in other parts of the world have made the same decision. Yet in some traditions, such as Lutheran, Anglican and some Reformed traditions of the Reformation period, evangelism has not always been prominent, when there was an assumption that church and nation were one and the same in an overarching 'Christendom' and therefore there was no need to convert the population. Even in recent times evangelism has been neglected by some parts of the church because of the existence of a culturally rooted Christendom or because the contemporary image of evangelism was a narrow and coercive one. For example, in the Introduction I described my own long-standing misgivings about the concept. The message from Mara region, however – a message that has come through loud and clear – is that a respectful and interactive form of evangelism needs to have a prominent role in any attempt to grow the church: it is the means by which the precious and wonderful gift of the gospel is clearly offered to those who do not yet have it. Therefore a second practical principle, reflecting a key dimension of church growth, is that *a deliberate and committed decision needs to be taken to make interactive evangelism a priority, in a structured and contextually respectful way.*

Is this possible in the British context? As with any initiative, it will depend on the way in which it is approached. To begin with, a decision needs to be taken to engage in it, whether at national or regional level by senior church leadership, whether by bishops or synods, or at local level by circuit or church councils. Common sense dictates, however, that those who make the decision need to be committed to putting it into practice. The case study revealed the huge commitment of lay people, pastors and the director of evangelism to the initiative: they were engaged in evangelism because they believed in it and wanted to extend it. This was key to its success. So the deliberate decision is probably best taken by those men and women at local level who will actually implement it. National and regional leadership can support and encourage evangelism, but the ones who need to take responsibility for making it happen are those at local level who will actually carry it out. The Church of England report *Setting God's People Free* (see above, pp. 90–1) echoes this sentiment in its call to invest in and entrust the laity with the mission of the church. A booklet recently posted to every parish in the Church of England from the Archbishops' Evangelism Task Group, *Evangelism for the Local Church*, also makes this point: evangelism is for the local church to put into practice and happens through the contacts that its people already have.

If, then, evangelism has a leading role in the whole enterprise, some questions immediately follow: *who* is to be evangelized, *how* are they to be approached and *what* is to be the content of this evangelism?

To answer the first of these it is worth recalling how the director of evangelism, before doing anything else, engaged in some sociological analysis and reflection. He asked which villages and groups of people did not yet have their own church, of any denomination. These would become the priority for his evangelism initiative. This highlights a need to study the demographics of a population and identify which groups will be approached. This might involve finding out who already has connections with churches, and avoiding them so as not to duplicate efforts. The key point is that evangelistic outreach is not to be a generalized approach to anyone who happens to live in an area, but to be geared towards specific groups of people who have been identified through local analysis, are then held in mind and heart throughout and who, honoured and respected and if responding with faith, will be entrusted with forming a new congregation and so numerically growing the organization of the church, one of the key dimensions of growth. In time, with support from the evangelism team and wider church, they will grow from the first to the second stage of congregational relations, from the donor–recipient relationship to the partnership relationship. A third practical principle, then, is that *evangelism needs to be for a chosen group of people who are honoured for who they are and kept at the centre of all that happens, and who, if they accept the grace of the gospel, will be entrusted with forming their own church and so extending the wider church.* There is a radical clarity about this principle: it is all about being very clear about who is being offered the gift of the gospel, and really handing it over to them if they accept it (rather than trying to hold on to it in some way after it has been offered). It picks up and expresses another key dimension of church growth: growth in congregational relationships.

In the British context one is able quite easily to analyse the demographics of a local area through government and local authority data available on the internet. It is also very necessary because many areas have a high population density and local churches often have links with a number of different groups. Decisions need to be made about which of these groups to approach if efforts are not to get dissipated by attempting to reach too many. The strategic focus and planning of Mara's director of evangelism provides a good example in this respect. (None of this, though, should make a church turn its back on those from other groups who choose to respond: all should be welcomed even if only one group is invited at any one time.)

This leads naturally into the question of *how* the approach is to be made. The Mara method begins, as we have seen, with being strategic in its planning of evangelism, identifying a specific group of people who will be approached. It then concentrates on an intensive period of lively events and invitations, which include preaching and teaching but also singing, dancing and film, adding an expressive and even sacramental dimension to the communication. In all this the communication is contextually appropriate to the culture and working lives of those people, and also includes interactive personal communication in their homes. The Mara approach to growth, then, is one of *the team offering the chosen group of people a special and intensive time of communication of the gospel through word and sacramental action, in appropriate, vivid and interactive ways.* This expression of the sacramental picks up another key dimension of church growth.

The booklet *Evangelism for the Local Church*, cited above, offers a simple and attractive way of practising intentional evangelism in the British context, one that 'is tried and tested, that can be applied in each church situation and is effective in introducing people to Jesus' (p. 3). It does this by help-fully separating out certain stages in the process, stages that are implicit in the Mara model, presenting them as a fourfold circular process. The first stage is 'contact', which happens through 'the initial relationships – probably already existing of those God has brought into your path' (p. 7). In Mara we saw this happening through community service. The second stage is 'nurture', which is 'an intentional investment in specific events that seek to grow the initial contact'. In Mara this happened in the initial stages of their evangelistic work. Third is 'commit-ment', which is 'the specific issuing of the invitation to people to follow Jesus Christ' (p. 7) through 'enabling a moment of "crisis" in which someone can respond to the gospel in a deci-sive and explicit way' (p. 12). In Mara this was a clear part of the evangelism. Finally comes 'growth': 'the development of the faith that has begun. In this way a person is grafted into the community of faith' (p. 7). In Mara this occurred through ongoing support of the new church by a local pastor and diocese. In *Evangelism for the Local Church* no timescale is given for these stages, so they can be enacted in whatever ways fit with the culture and working lives of the people concerned. This reflects the way that British people are usually cautious about committing to new ways of life, and that trust has to be built through 'nurture' before any kind of invitation will be accepted. The timescale for evangelism, in other words, will be much longer than a week.

The Mara approach clarifies and sharpens this model in at least three ways: it highlights the way 'initial contact' can be through community service; it suggests a sharper strategic dimension in the way it shows the evangelism team identifying a specific group of people who will be approached in a contextually respectful way; and it emphasizes the role of personal interaction in which enquirers have the opportunity to question and discuss the offer in a one-to-one format – a significant investment of time on the part of the team.

But what is to be the content of evangelism? This is a key question about the way the gospel should interact with the society and culture of those being evangelized. In Mara's evangelism we saw how this was approached in two ways.

The first was through prior examination of the local culture in order to work out how to present the gospel. We saw how this difficult task was approached in a relatively simple way, by identifying those aspects of the culture that were obviously opposed to the gospel, such as FGM, gender inequality and the harmful way women and children were treated, and then showing how becoming a believer involves abandoning these practices and living in a different way. But this was not the same as a general condemnation of the culture: this was not implied by this approach, which after all used evangelists from that same culture, who would largely work within and validate their culture. This contextually sensitive approach could therefore be described as one of presenting the gospel in a way that would *reform* rather than *replace* the culture of the people who come to faith (in contrast to earlier colonial approaches), leading to an indigenous discipleship. It generates another practical principle, which is that *the team should not flinch from challenging aspects of a society and culture that are obviously opposed to the gospel, while generally affirming the culture of that society as far as possible, leading to an indigenous discipleship for those who come to faith*. This picks up and expresses another dimension of church growth, growth in discipleship.

When applying this principle to a Western context such as in Britain, a clear difficulty is to find agreement among Christians about what aspects of its culture and society are obviously opposed to the gospel. The sanctioning of gay marriage is one that some Christians affirm while others condemn, as is abortion beyond a limited number of weeks. But there are other aspects of contemporary society that most would condemn, such as the high level of child poverty, lack of provision for the homeless and increasingly high rates of isolation and loneliness. An evangelism that includes condemnation of these kinds of features of British society and culture, and commitment to fight them, will have the same kind of edge found in evangelism in Mara region.

The second 'content' feature of Mara evangelism, at the heart of the whole process, was the telling of the story of Jesus, from his birth through his ministry to his death and resurrection as Son of God and Saviour of the world, with an invitation to commit to faith. This shows the power and importance of telling and retelling the gospel story. But we also saw how this was done through showing the Jesus film. This may seem culturally inappropriate, as it is an American film rather than being African produced. But the version shown was dubbed into Swahili and follows the gospel accounts very closely. It clearly caught the attention of its audience, generating widespread and heartfelt responses. It shows how evangelism can sometimes get help from beyond the local culture, such as through a film, to great effect, providing a fresh perspective that catches people's imagination and builds their faith, like the foreign particle of sand in the oyster that enables a pearl to grow. The resulting practical principle, then, is that *at the heart of everything that happens, the gospel story of Jesus' life, death and resurrection as Son of God and Saviour of the world, the greatest story in the world, will need to be told with fresh creativity and inspiration, not afraid to get help from beyond the local culture, and as an invitation to faith and discipleship.*

In the British context what would this mean? It is a tough challenge because of the way we are saturated with different media and styles of storytelling. The use of a slightly dated and low-budget feature film, such as the Jesus film, would simply not generate the same response as it has done in the villages of Tanzania. Furthermore, the generational divides in our society probably mean that different age groups will need different kinds of storytelling, making it impossible to provide one version suitable for all. Creativity and imagination will be needed, guided by a prayerful attitude that is open to the promptings of the Spirit and attentive to scripture. But in the same way that Mara evangelism drew on the help of a film from a very different culture, so British evangelism might draw on the help of different and unconventional ways of telling the gospel story.

Lucy Moore provides some pointers from the context of Messy Church towards how this could happen. While she is writing about how to put on liturgy, her words are equally applicable to evangelism and especially on telling the gospel story:

> Any actor can tell you how fatally easy it is for a script to be killed by a lack of understanding or commitment to engage with it … As a storyteller will tell you, knowing a story by heart would demonstrate that the teller cares enough about the story to have internalized it and made it part of them: a book just gets between the teller and the listener. A musician may take a score on stage. An actor doesn't. It cramps their communication, because their communication involves the visual and the kinaesthetic as well as the auditory. In the challenge of a Messy Church context, where there is little learned 'good behaviour' in the congregation (and anecdotal evidence suggests most 'inappropriate behaviour' comes from adults rather than children!), powerful communication is crucial and every creative resource is needed to share the 'story' effectively. Reading from a book won't cut the mustard. The story is worth more than that. Messy Church gives the challenge of sharing the story with fresh creativity with a new generation. (Potter and Mobsby 2017, pp. 108–9)

Here, then, is some clarification about the initial practical principles of Mara growth, picking up and expressing all six dimensions of the ecology of church growth described in earlier chapters. With each principle there has also been some description of how it could be put into practice in the British context. In summary, the principles are as follows, recognizing that they need to be put into practice as a whole rather than picked up in a piecemeal way:

1 Before anything else, the church needs to be actively engaged in serving its community in a contextually appropriate and committed way.
2 A deliberate and committed decision then needs to be taken to make interactive evangelism a priority, in a structured and contextually respectful way.
3 This will need to be for a chosen group of people who are honoured for who they are and kept at the centre of all that happens, and who, if they accept the grace of the gospel, will be entrusted with forming their own church and so extending the wider church.
4 The evangelism team will offer the chosen group of people a special and intensive time of communication of the gospel through word and sacramental action, in appropriate, vivid and interactive ways.
5 The team should not flinch from challenging aspects of a society and culture that are obviously opposed to the gospel, while generally affirming the culture of that society as far as possible, leading to an indigenous discipleship for those who come to faith.
6 At the heart of all of this, the gospel story of Jesus' life, death and resurrection as Son of God and Saviour of the world, the greatest story in the world, will need to be told with fresh creativity and inspiration, not afraid to get help from beyond the local culture, and as an invitation to faith and discipleship.

Could these principles be put into practice as a whole by a team of people? This would clearly be challenging, requiring motivational leadership and ongoing commitment, but nothing has been suggested above that shows it is impossible as such. What is needed is a clear commitment from the start, first to serving the most pressing needs of the local community and then to deliberate evangelism. This will need clarity about who is being approached, how they will be approached and what they will be entrusted with, along with a hard-headed commitment to be challenging on some aspects of the local culture and creative and imaginative with others in order to communicate the grace of the gospel and its life-giving invitation.

5

Bringing Mara Growth Home

Into Local Schools

What would expressing these principles as a whole look like in the Northern context, especially for a fairly typical medium-sized local church in a provincial town facing the steep challenge of trying to grow in an increasingly post-Christian society? The Mara approach to growth, as we have seen, is an organic one, meaning that growth is not manufactured through an instrumental process but must be cultivated in an interactive and responsive way, like nurturing crops in a vegetable garden. What would this mean in this very different setting?

The following pages give one answer to this question, drawing on a case study of one church that has responded creatively and responsively to the challenge of needing to grow. It is not the only answer and readers may know of other churches in other settings that provide better illustrations of Mara growth. But here is an example that can begin to put flesh and blood on the dry bones of the principles described above, helping us to complete the move from theory to practice.

Some of the following may seem a world away from Tanzania, which of course it is. We need to recognize the social and cultural reasons why church growth will not have the same appearance as in Mara. These will include people's unwillingness in urban areas to let others into their homes, suspicious attitudes to religion fed by child abuse scandals, the stereotypical view of religion and science being in opposition, the traditional view of religion as a private matter not to be discussed openly, the fact that many older people in Britain already have strong preconceptions about what church is, and its association with the state and with conventionality. All these factors, and others, will mean that church growth will look differently from the way it looks in Mara, not least in its pace and intensity. (See Andrew Walls, *The Missionary Movement in Christian History*, for a discussion of the different rates of church growth in different places in different eras.) However, the book has gone behind the outward expressions of growth in Tanzania to the underlying elements, and identified what they are. The earlier chapters have revealed no fewer than six dimensions of growth, with three stages of growth within each dimension, and a number of practical principles needed to implement it. These elements have already been found to be present in the British context, in different places among different groups, providing important points of connection between the two contexts. These now allow us to explore how 'Mara growth' as a whole might be expressed by a local church here.

The following case study shows how a congregation grew through a developing relationship with its surrounding community over a four-year period. It is not so much a history of the church within that period as a narrative of one important facet of the life of that church, its mission and growth in several dimensions.

Setting the Scene

The church building, a high and spacious structure built in the early Victorian era and enlarged at the start of the twentieth century, is located near the centre of a small town in the north of England. The town is typical of many across the country with a largely white British population of working families and retired people. Employment is in local schools, hospitals, light industry and the service sector. Income levels range from low to medium, with some households struggling with multiple deprivation, many managing to hold their own, and a few being quite wealthy. Social isolation, among the young as well as the old, is an increasing feature of the culture of the town, though a local tradition of social clubs and sports clubs helps to counteract this to some extent.

The church is located near the centre of the town but not in an especially visible way. In the past it had a civic role when the town had its own local council and the town hall looked to the parish church for ceremonial functions, filling the large building with hundreds of worshippers on special occasions. But this role has largely disappeared, apart from hosting an annual Remembrance Day service, and the regular congregation at the start of the four-year period was much like those of many other local churches in the area, averaging between 50 and 80 adults (plus a small group of children) on an ordinary Sunday, though increasingly tending to the lower rather than the upper end of this scale. It was, according to Steve Croft's typology, a 'pastoral church' of between 50 and 100 adult members, lying between the 'family church' of up to 50 members, and the 'programme church' of 100 to 300 adults (Croft 1999, pp. 194–6). In this way it was typical of a large number of ordinary churches across the country. Without its civic role the church had become, in effect, a voluntary association of retired people, with some younger families and single people, broadly reflecting the demographic of the area, though with a higher proportion of retired to working people than the wider population, and with a slightly higher income level than the town's average. The style of worship was of a traditional character, based on the Eucharist, with a small robed choir, monthly contemporary worship led by a music group, and a range of social activities through the year that built up a sense of community among its members. The wider community came to the church for baptisms and funerals, and an occasional wedding.

After-School Clubs

Noticing that the size of the congregation was steadily diminishing, despite a number of initiatives over the years, the church council decided that it was time for a new approach to outreach. If the local population was no longer coming to the church, it bravely resolved that the church must 'go to them'. It decided to do this through two nearby primary schools with which it had a connection (Church of England primary schools, where the church council had the right to nominate a number of school governors and the clergy and lay ministers took assemblies on a regular basis). These schools provided valuable points of contact between the congregation and a large number of young families. One of the clergy, an older and disabled curate with energy and vision, inspired the church council to take the bold decision to run some after-school clubs in the schools on four days of the week. The church would provide volunteer helpers to help run the clubs and the church council subsequently decided to employ a children's worker to plan the activities and take a lead, not least organizing the dedicated group of volunteers, some of whom were recruited from beyond the congregation and so helped to swell the number of adults involved in church work generally. The clubs were to be fun and lively, within a broadly Christian ethos, with a 'circle time' at the end with a thought and a prayer. They were not set up with the ulterior motive of recruiting new members into the congregation but were to be for their own sake, to provide local children and their families, some of whom were living in households of multiple deprivation, with fun and friendly support.

These clubs were an immediate success, building up to a combined membership of around 60 children. The volunteers described how much they enjoyed being part of them and how they felt that they got even more out of them than what they put in.

This initiative, which began before the start of the four-year period and continued throughout it, is therefore a clear example of a church deciding to serve its surrounding community and doing so in an effective way. It showed that the church was genuinely committed to loving and caring for the people among whom it was placed without any ulterior motive of seeking to possess them. In the way they were planned and followed through, the after-school clubs demonstrated that the church had grown from the first to the second stage of community service: from occasional acts of service to a singular act of planned and committed service over a number of years (see above, Chapter 3).

To Messy Church

What of the other dimensions of church growth? Community service is a presupposition of the other dimensions rather than a substitute for them, so much more was needed. The church council began to wonder how the children attending the after-school clubs, and their parents, might be drawn into church and nurtured in the Christian faith. It wisely recognized that the Sunday morning Eucharist was too long and too passive for these children and their parents. It therefore decided to start a weekday Messy Church (see above, pp. 67–9, 81–2), for children and their parents, which would meet in the church building after school and replace the after-school clubs for a week at a time, initially once a term. The children's worker would again coordinate the event, with additional support from the church's ministry team. Hot food would be provided by the church at the beginning of the session, followed by a range of craft activities and games around a Christian theme, and finishing with a simple 'celebration' in the sanctuary area of the church, which would close the event with a song, talk and prayer. The food would be served free of charge, as an act of hospitality, and the crafts and games would be suitable for the broad age range of children that would attend, picking up seasonal themes as a way of expressing Christian teaching, such as Christmas, Easter, Harvest and Remembrance. The celebration at the end would give simple and clear teaching that explained the themes, adding words to the actions of the activities, before inviting the children and parents to make their own response to God in the song and prayers.

Once again, this initiative was immediately successful, with an average of 80 attending. Children and parents would come bustling into the church when the doors opened, with the provision of the meal meaning that parents were not anxious to get their children home for tea. The crafts appealed more to some of the children and the games more to others. It was fortunate that the church chairs could be cleared to one side of the building to create an open space for the activities. The celebration time came at a moment when the children were happy to settle down and be quiet after all the action. The helpers entered enthusiastically into the activities at each session despite being weary by the end, with the setting up, the catering and the clearing up. As the Messy Church gatherings became more established the organizers were able to start recruiting parents into the group of helpers, so easing the pressure on the initial volunteers, though more were needed.

This initiative shows growth in three of the dimensions of church growth identified in the table above (see p. 93). First, the inviting of local children and parents into the church for Christian hospitality, fellowship, teaching and worship shows evangelistic communication beginning to take place. The church was opening its doors and sharing its beliefs in an open and enjoyable way that avoided any sense of judgementalism or coercion sometimes found in more traditional forms of evangelism. Interactive communication was taking place, around craft tables and through games, of Christian values and beliefs, with the sharing of simple teaching at the end of the event. This was possible through the volunteers being able to talk to the children on a one-to-one basis around the tables while getting on with the activities, showing growth from the uni-vocal to the interactive stage within this dimension of church growth.

Second, through the meal and the activities the Messy Church meetings were providing effective signs of the beliefs they were seeking to express. In the eating together, making things together, joining in with games related to the overall theme and singing at the end there was opportunity to experience in multi-sensory ways what was being communicated. A sacrament, as we have seen, is basically a physical sign that helps to bring into effect the thing it is pointing to, and here there were some effective signs of the Christian faith. This was, in other words, sacramental expression, albeit in informal ways. The teaching at the end of the meeting was crucial; through the words of the speaker, it provided meaning to identify the experience, a ministry of word complementing a ministry of sacrament. This feature illustrates growth from the spontaneous stage to the intentional stage of the sacramental dimension, because Messy Church is designed to combine word and action in this way.

Third, Messy Church encouraged growth in congregational relationships, because now that a significant number of the congregation were welcoming a crowd of children and adults into their building and providing hospitality for them, they were having to become a mutually supportive team working in partnership with each other. They were no longer coming to the building just to receive the ministry of others, principally the clergy and other worship leaders on a Sunday morning, but were becoming co-leaders, in partnership with each other and the ministry team, standing shoulder to shoulder in their commitment, enthusiasm and fatigue, and so building up their common life. In this they had also moved into the second stage of growth, from the donor–recipient stage to the partnership stage of congregational relationships.

But what of growth in discipleship, leading ultimately to numerical growth in the membership of the church? Here, unfortunately, the evidence was not very strong. After a couple of years of running Messy Church it was not clear that any of the children and their parents had made commitments to following Christ. The meetings were boisterous and fun and good for all the reasons mentioned above, but they lacked a consistent way of supporting individuals in their faith journey. There was little opportunity for adults to follow through conversations with children from one meeting to the next. It was hard to see how discipleship, another key dimension of church growth, was being nurtured.

To Godly Play

After reviewing the meetings and reflecting on what was needed the church council decided that a further step should be taken, to build on what was already happening. This was to send another children's worker back into the schools, this time during class time, with the support of the head teachers, to run 'Godly Play' sessions for some designated classes. Funds would be raised to pay this worker for two days a week. They would work with the schools to develop a schedule of sessions with half a class at a time, and would gather together the necessary resources for the storytelling at the heart of Godly Play. Before examining what happened, it is important to recognize how the church council was being flexible and responsive in its approach to growth. It was acknowledging that its previous initiatives were not enough, and that while its commitment to Messy Church was maintained there was a need to supplement this with something more. This illustrates an organic approach, to cultivating growth in different ways at different moments depending on the changing needs of the context. Growth, then, was being nurtured not manufactured, another important connection with Mara growth.

Godly Play is a methodology for children's work in church influenced by Montessori educational theory (which is a child-centred, holistic education developed by Maria Montessori in Italy in the first half of the twentieth century). It was conceived by an American priest, Jerome W. Berryman, who described it in the following way: 'the goal of this approach to religious education is not to transfer answers or facts ... It is to teach the art of *using* religious language to make meaning and find direction in life and death' (Berryman 1995, p. 63, italics original). The relevance to discipleship is clear from this definition because the learner has as much of a creative role as the teacher and it is focused on goals and aims in life. By 'religious language' Berryman seems to imply not just words but the whole system of symbolic and associated meanings that are found within the Christian tradition and scriptures.

He emphasizes being able to use this whole system: 'the goal of Godly Play is for children to enter adolescence with an inner working model of the Christian language system at their disposal' (p. 91).

This experiential approach to learning uses a range of simple handmade props, such as figures, blocks, sand, shapes and models to help tell the story and encourage personal response to it by the learner. There is a distinctive role for the leader, which seems counter to most understandings of leading children's work: they should 'model how to "enter" into the flow and metaphor of the lesson. Avoid eye contact with the children unless necessary so they can focus on the lesson and not on the presenter' (Berryman 1995, p. 91). Those who see Godly Play in action often report on how effective this is, even in a large group of excitable children who are not familiar with church: their attention to the story is often total.

Back with our case study, the Godly Play sessions in the schools would have just two adults present, with the children in small groups, settled into a peaceful and quiet 'Godly Play space'. The children would be given time and space to experience and express their own spiritual awareness and questions. Unlike in Messy Church there was extended opportunity for the leaders to sit alongside the children and have ongoing conversations with them while the children engaged in the activities. This is in accord with Berryman's guidance for the leaders, that 'to enable the group to be more creative and alive, one must become the servant of the group and almost disappear in it ... This means that the art they learn, the experience of community, and the experience of God, is theirs' (Berryman 1995, p. 90).

This approach is seen in the use of open questions and 'wondering'. At certain moments the leader looks to the children for answers, and at others leaves questions for everyone to think about. Berryman states that the 'learning mentor ... models how to wonder ... shows ... invites' (Berryman 1995, p. 22).

Godly Play offers free rein to respond to stories using a variety of creative media, opening access to creative learning that is beneficial to all ages: 'the multi-sensory approach helps children and adults gain access to the lesson at whatever stage of cognitive development they may be using' (Berryman 1995, p. 44). Sessions include refreshments, which are taken together as children and adults sit in a circle, a moment that can acquire a sacramental sense. The 'focal point of the room shows Christ at the centre' (p. 82).

With the case study, the plan for the children's worker was to aim to reach all the classes in the schools over a two-year period, allowing contact with up to 400 children.

Once the sessions had begun, the Godly Play leader reported back that the children had not only taken part in the sessions with enthusiasm and commitment but had sometimes demonstrated a depth of spiritual awareness and questioning that took her breath away! This had happened in more than one of the groups. The storytelling and 'wondering' were drawing out of the children profound and wonderful insights in conversation and some heartfelt responses to God in the prayer time. Here, then, was something that Messy Church had not been able to provide: a direct encounter with God on a personal basis and the planting of seeds of discipleship in the hearts and minds of these children.

It is important to see how the Godly Play initiative was fulfilling many of the practical principles identified in the previous chapter. It was building on the church's community service and especially its after-school clubs in the schools, which had already given the church a good relationship with the staff, pupils and parents of the schools. It arose out of a deliberate decision to reach the children in a structured and contextually respectful way (fulfilling the second principle). It kept the needs of the child at the centre of all that happened, as Berryman and Montessori require (fulfilling the first part of the third principle). The leaders gave the children special and intensive times for communicating the gospel, through the storytelling, in actions as well as words, and in an interactive way (fulfilling the fourth principle). It implicitly challenged contemporary culture by replacing a hierarchical 'leader and led' model of community life with a circular model in which the leader sits among the children and avoids dominating their outlook (fulfilling the fifth principle in a small but important way). And it told the gospel story with wonder and awe, in vivid and multi-sensory ways, keeping Christ at 'the centre of the room' (fulfilling the sixth principle).

What the initiative did not do is issue an invitation to ongoing commitment and discipleship. It was not possible to do this in a school environment, as anything resembling proselytism is not allowed. The sessions had to be open-ended, without an altar call, as it were. So while the seeds of discipleship were planted in the hearts and minds of the children, the opportunity to move from the enquiry stage to the apprenticeship stage was not there. Also, in practical terms any follow-up was very difficult as the children were not going to come to church on a Sunday morning because the weekend routines and expectations of their families would not allow it and, indeed, the children would lose contact with the Godly Play leader when they moved on to secondary school. The discipleship aims of the third, fifth and sixth principles, then, were not fulfilled.

The Missing Piece

It could be argued that this did not matter. The influential South African missiologist David Bosch wrote in 1991 that mission 'can not simply be the planting of churches or the saving of souls; rather, it has to be service of the *missio Dei* [mission of God]'. This

affects all people in all aspects of their existence. Mission is God's turning to the world in respect of creation, care, redemption and consummation ... It takes place in ordinary human history, not exclusively in and through the church ... The *missio Dei* is God's activity, which embraces both the church and the world, and in which the church may be privileged to participate. (Bosch 1991, p. 391)

This perspective suggests that any growth within people of their capacity to connect with God, in the community, in schools or hospitals or elsewhere, as much as in the church, is a step forward for mission and something for the church to celebrate. The goal of mission, by implication, is not growth in the size of the instrument of that mission, the church, but the growth of God's kingdom of faith, hope and love in the world at large.

Such a perspective is supported by the recognition that the pursuit of numerical growth of congregations for its own sake could be a hiding to nothing. Contemporary British culture has moved away from the whole notion of signing up to formal membership of local organizations with regular attendance at meetings. Sociologists have for some time been pointing out that membership of many attendance-based voluntary organizations, from political parties and trade unions through to team sports and village institutes, has been in decline. These have relied on a sense of obligation to the organization among their members, but British and indeed Western culture in general is experiencing a widespread transition from a culture of obligation to a culture of consumption. In this setting the churches have fared better than most, seeing their membership decline much less quickly than other organizations, something that should be noted and celebrated. Nevertheless, the trajectory for formal church membership will be one of continuing decline, despite pockets of growth in church attendance in urban areas arising from immigration and from church planting by a few big churches. The tide of culture is flowing strongly in one direction. A pressing question is whether churches are to try to resist this, becoming more and more counter-cultural and possibly sectarian, or whether they are to embrace contemporary culture, become more inculturated and find different ways for Christian faith and life to come to expression.

The sociologist Linda Woodhead has indicated how the latter might take place. Writing in the *Church Times* (2015), she calls for attention to be given to the church's entry-points into society, those places where the rubber of Christianity meets the road of real life: in homes, playgroups, schools, and other places where children are socialized; in the occasional Offices of christenings, weddings and funerals, and the new personal and civic rituals that are developing; in railway stations, shopping centres, hospitals, and other sites of chaplaincy; in our built heritage, and in cherished traditions.

Chaplaincy, in its various manifestations, will be central to this.

This would shift the aim of church growth away from a congregational focus and to a society-wide focus, of helping the wider community to be touched and transformed by God's salvation, becoming yeast that leavens the dough of society. So a church's primary call would not be to recruit others to join its regular membership, but to become an agent of change in the wider community and, especially, in turning the hearts and minds of the population to the things of God and his kingdom. This would involve every aspect of a congregation's life, through all their interactions with their community through home life and work as well as Sunday services, helping the wider population connect with God's mission in the world. It would see them fully embracing the famous saying of Archbishop William Temple, that the church is the only organization that exists for the sake of those who are not its members.

The Mara approach to growth would not dispute the immense value and importance of helping congregations, chaplains and others making connections in these ways. It would see them falling naturally within the service dimension of church growth – the church serving the needs of society at large, especially of the need to reconnect society with the kingdom of God. However, as we have seen, it would not regard this as sufficient. As discussed through all the chapters of this book, church growth is multi-dimensional, and some of the dimensions specifically concern the growth of the congregation, in numbers, in relationships, in sacramental expression and in discipleship. The need for growth in these dimensions makes us return to the importance and role of cultivating and nurturing the life of the local church.

In relation to this important point the case study has revealed an example of church growth in Britain that is in accord with the core principles of Mara growth in nearly all respects. The after-school clubs showed the church laying a strong foundation of serving the local community in a singular and committed way; the running of Messy Church showed growth in interactive and sacramental communication taking place with a large number of children and their parents over several years; the team work required to put on Messy Church showed growth in congregational relationships towards a real sense of partnership; the provision of Godly Play sessions in local schools showed the development of evangelistic and sacramental communication in deep and moving ways with some children responding with faith and trust. However, by the end of the four years there was something still missing, a crucial aspect of church growth had not yet taken place: the growth of discipleship among the children, taking those who were interested from the enquiry stage to the apprenticeship stage. Unlike in Mara, new believers were not being formed into their own new congregation in which they would journey forward in their discipleship. Godly Play participants, in other words, were not being offered a way of becoming members of the body of Christ. Some stepping stones were missing, including the means of allowing them to move from being young enquirers to becoming apprentices in the way of Christ.

What would this link be? Based on youth ministry in other places, it is clear there would need to be a safe and relaxed meeting place, accessible and secure, which the young people could make their own. They would need to be allowed to meet at a time that suited them and have access to refreshments. But unlike youth clubs in general this gathering would have a direction of travel, from exploring discipleship to embracing faith and commitment. It would be a place where those young people who had previously been participating in Godly Play could gather, support each other, have fun and explore their faith.

Michael Moynagh provides some helpful guidance on how discipleship can be nurtured in what would become a new ecclesial community:

> Whatever the pathway ... putting in signposts to Jesus will help people who want to do so to move from 'Building community' to 'Exploring discipleship'. These signposts should be sensitive to where people are on their spiritual quests; signposts pointing to the next stage will generally be more encouraging than ones that invite a giant leap. Equally, signposts should give permission rather than exert pressure. They should offer scenic options rather than compulsory detours: 'Here's a route you might like to follow' rather than 'This is where you must go.' In a culture that values choice, signposts expand the options available to people. They present opportunities to explore spirituality that individuals may not have found elsewhere. (Moynagh 2017, p. 48)

Moynagh provides some examples of such signposts, including baking cakes and giving them away to households in the neighbourhood, putting up prayer boards for prayer requests, baby massage and prayer sessions for mothers and their babies, cafe breakfasts with short prayer sessions, and open sessions in the run-up to Christmas with seasonal activities and a short talk on the meaning of Christmas.

Nevertheless, the Mara approach emphasizes the need for such signposts to have a sense of purpose and direction and to invite a committed response; in other words, to include the offer of the freedom and grace of the gospel of Christ with the possibility of responding in faith, commitment and discipleship. A longer-term aim would be for the group to become a new ecclesial community or in traditional language, a church. As in Mara, the young people would need to be trusted with forming the life and character of their congregation, an exciting and daunting project, while also being sensitively supported by adult partners from the parent church. Over time and at their own pace, through exploring Scripture and Christian tradition, they would find out what it means to be the body of Christ in an organic kind of way. According to the Mara approach they would come to nominate their own leadership and at the right time be prepared for the formal sacraments of baptism, confirmation and the Eucharist by clergy and other ministers from the parent church. Ongoing mentoring would be needed to bring them to this point. It would take longer than in Mara because, as we have seen, for various reasons faith journeys in Western culture are often slower than elsewhere.

If this missing piece were to be in place, then all the practical principles of Mara growth, covering the six dimensions of church growth, would have found expression in this place. As the parent church congregation continued to diminish in size, it could rejoice that a new congregation was being brought to life to take forward the Christian presence in that neighbourhood for the next generation. Over time the new congregation would itself grow and come to maturity, eventually incorporating the older congregation when both were ready to combine their life and move forward together.

Conclusion

God Gives the Growth

'I planted, Apollos watered, but God gave the growth' (1 Corinthians 3.6). These words of Paul have prompted this book to offer an organic analogy for church growth, that of the growth of a tree from the germination of its seed through to its maturity: growth that takes place in a number of ways all at once. These words now remind us of another key point, that it is not the evangelists that generate church growth but God himself. This is an especially important insight in the wake of the previous chapter, which was all about a church council taking the initiative in a strategically planned, dynamic and committed way. The council could easily have assumed that once it had completed its initiatives it should keep managing and controlling the subsequent life of the new young Christians and their nascent church. But, paradoxically, this is not what they are to do. They are to let God be God, for it is God who gives the growth, as the new Christians of Mara discovered many times over. In the words of the psalm:

By awesome deeds you answer us with deliverance,
  O God of our salvation;
you are the hope of all the ends of the earth
  and of the farthest seas. (Psalm 65.5)

This should come as no surprise. The organic analogy itself suggests that once the seed is planted, other processes come into play. The planting may be done by a gardener or farmer, but then nature takes over and the germination and growth of the seedlings will happen in its own time. The gardener must be patient and trusting. So, as Paul reminds us, the growth of God's church will happen in God's own way and time. Again as the psalm puts it:

You visit the earth and water it,
    you greatly enrich it;
the river of God is full of water;
    you provide the people with grain,
    for so you have prepared it.
You water its furrows abundantly,
    settling its ridges,
softening it with showers,
    and blessing its growth. (Psalm 65.9–10)

For a church council, or ministry team, or Godly Play leader, people used to being in charge, this may be hard to accept. But it can be liberating in that it shows that once they have played their part they are not responsible for what subsequently happens or fails to happen. Mission belongs to God as the *missio Dei* and this can release his people to concentrate on the particular parts they have to play within its wider unfolding life.

The analogy highlights some other aspects of growth. The first comes from noticing different growing conditions in different parts of the world, such as the contrast between the tropics and northern latitudes. In those places where there is warmth, rainfall and good soil, growth can be quick and abundant. The conditions are conducive and the farmer will see rich yields from his or her planting. But in northern climes, where there is less warmth and perhaps the soil is less fertile, growth is slower and yields will be less. In the same way, the analogy suggests, mission and evangelism will yield different results in different places. As we have already seen, the level of receptivity of the people being approached will be different in different locations, and the degree to which they accept the offer of God's grace and come together to form their own churches will vary from place to place. In Mara region over the last 30 years the conditions in this tropical part of the world have been especially propitious. In many parts of the global North they are currently not very propitious, though the fresh expressions movement is bucking the trend on this. The different levels of receptivity should not take evangelists by surprise and they should not blame themselves when there is a low uptake (or, alternatively, think that a high uptake is all down to them). They are entrusting the gospel to others, a process of 'self-donation' (Moynagh 2017, p. 409), and so what happens next is up to those who receive it and to their degree of openness to God's grace.

Another insight of the analogy comes from the way a gardener or farmer, once they have planted the seeds, will not completely abandon them. Weeding needs to take place, as does protection of the plot or field from wild animals, and sometimes irrigation is necessary. The space and conditions within which growth can take place need protecting and maintaining by cultivation. In the same way the conditions within which a new church will grow and flourish need maintaining, which may include the upkeep of the physical space where the church meets, safeguarding its members and providing nourishment through the sacraments, teaching and institutional support from the wider church. In Mara it was the role of the priest in the nearest parish to provide this support, helping to teach and guide the people towards baptism, confirmation, Holy Communion and the constitution of their church into a parish. In other contexts, new young churches also need ongoing support from the wider church, for encouragement, guidance, connectivity through sacramental ministry and the means to become a full member of the wider Catholic church. In many cases this will come from the home church that sent out the initial evangelism team in the first place. It is currently estimated that three-quarters of fresh expressions in England have come out of the parish churches of the Church of England, so these will be the bodies that provide this kind of external support in a partnership relationship (see Jackson 2015, pp. 168–9).

But growth has not one but six different dimensions, so how can this support be provided in a way that encourages all dimensions? Yet another feature of the organic analogy can help here, in the way a gardener or farmer will pay attention to the whole life of the plant or crop and tailor their intervention to its current needs, whether it be through weeding or fencing or irrigation. Sensitivity and flexibility are the order of the day, based on the wisdom of experience. In the same way, those responsible for the support of new churches need to be sensitive to every dimension of their growth, in community relationships, sacramental expression, community service, discipleship and organizational form, as well as in the initial evangelism, and encourage growth in all areas. This is where the summary table presented above (see p. 93) comes into its own, for it can be used as a template to audit the life of a church, identifying the dimensions in which there is mature growth and those dimensions where growth has yet to take place. Areas will then be revealed where time and energy need to be given to encourage that growth. Churches will usually have experienced more growth in some areas than in others. The task, then, is to put in place conditions that foster growth in the dimensions where growth is especially needed. What this means in practice will depend on what needs to be done for those people in their own context: there is no one-size-fits-all set of answers, and support teams need to be able to draw on experience.

The analogy also points to the way that growth is not instantaneous, like the construction of a new car rolling off the production line, but is an organic process that takes place in stages throughout life, from birth through to maturity. The table, then, is a tool not just for fresh expressions but for all churches that have a desire to grow. It can be used to review the life of ancient parish churches and cathedrals as well new ecclesial communities. All churches can continue to grow if they have the intention to do so and are given the opportunity. They may not be able to grow in one or two dimensions at a certain time, for reasons outside their control, but that still leaves four or five others for them to work on. Leaders can review the whole life of the church in their care and see in which areas growth is needed and possible, and then work to put in place the conditions to allow that growth to take place.

Finally, though, it is again important to remember that it is God who gives the growth and therefore leadership must be 'put in its place' within the bigger picture of God's mission and of his leadership. In Mara this was apparent when pastors and lay ministers talked about the need to take a 'spiritual approach', based upon prayer by the team throughout the week of evangelism, with a key element of the preaching being the offer of God's reconciliation over and above anything offered by the team. A larger dimension, then, was being brought into play, which was the presence and action of God himself, rather than just relying on the efforts and activities of the team.

Akiri continues:

In other words, the role of those involved in evangelism is to share God's love (John 3.16), and leave it to the Lord of the harvest to do what he wills, knowing that the harvest is always plentiful (Matthew 9.37–38). Matthew also shows an aspect of church growth that should be emphasized: prayer for growth. Growth does not happen simply due to elaborate strategies and human effort. It happens also because the people of God and church leaders pray for growth.

This prayer is anchored in the teaching of the Bible about the purpose of Jesus coming into the world. He came into the world to save sinners (Matthew 1.21) and there is salvation in no one else except Jesus (Acts 4.12) and that those who call on his name will be saved (Romans 10.13).

What Mara region bishops, pastors and lay ministers and others in the African church do is to obey what Jesus said in the Great Commission: 'Go and make disciples' (Matthew 28.19–20; cf. John 20.21).

Those who obey the command and go are messengers of God who know that people have to be given the opportunity to call upon the name of Lord, but as Paul says, 'How are they to call on him in whom they have not believed? And how are they to believe in him whom they have not heard?

And how are they to hear without someone preaching? And how are they to preach without being sent? As it is written, "How beautiful are the feet of those who preach the good news"' (Romans 10.14–15).

Leadership, in other words, is not merely a human project but ultimately comes from the divine life of the Trinity. The growing and flourishing of the church, the concern of this book as a whole, is a divine gift, like the growing and flourishing of crops or of a great oak tree, so God needs to be invited to play his part and the outcome entrusted into his hands. Then in God's good time the church will be able to pray with the psalmist that

> You crown the year with your bounty;
>   your wagon tracks overflow with richness.
> The pastures of the wilderness overflow,
>   the hills gird themselves with joy,
> the meadows clothe themselves with flocks,
>   the valleys deck themselves with grain,
>   they shout and sing together for joy. (Psalm 65.11–13)

References and Further Reading

Akiri, R. M. (1999) *The Growth of Christianity in Central Tanzania: A Socio-Historical Analysis of the Role of Indigenous Agents 1876–1933*, unpublished PhD thesis, Edinburgh University.

Archbishops' Evangelism Task Group (2017) *Evangelism for the Local Church*, Church of England.

Berryman, J. (1995) *Godly Play: An Imaginative Approach to Religious Education*, Minneapolis, MN: Augsburg.

Berryman, J. (2009) *Teaching Godly Play: How to Mentor the Spiritual Development of Children*, Denver, CO: Morehouse.

Bonhoeffer, D. (1971) *Letters and Papers from Prison*, ed. E. Bethge, enlarged edition, London: SCM Press.

The Book of Common Prayer 1662, 2nd Standard Edition (2004), Cambridge: Cambridge University Press.

Booker, M. and Ireland, M. (2003) *Evangelism – Which Way Now?* London: Church House Publishing.

Bosch, D. J. (1991) *Transforming Mission: Paradigm Shifts in Theology of Mission*, Maryknoll, NY: Orbis Books.

Browne, R. in (2013) *The Writings of Robert Harrison and Robert Browne*, Elizabethan Non-Conformist Texts, Vol. II: ed. L. H. Carlson and A. Peel, London: Routledge.

Cameron, H. (2010) *Resourcing Mission*, London: SCM Press.

Cameron, H. and Marashi, M. (2004) *Form or Substance in the Learning and Skills Sector: Does Organizational Form Affect Learning Outcomes?* London: Learning and Skills Development Agency.

Centre for Theology and Community (2016a) *Love, Sweat and Tears*, London: Centre for Theology and Community.

Centre for Theology and Community (2016b) *Church Growth in East London*, London: Centre for Theology and Community.

Church of England (2017) *Setting God's People Free*, GS 2056, at: www.churchofengland.org/sites/default/files/2017-11/GS%20Misc%202056%20Setting%20God%27s%20People%20Free.pdf

Church of England (2011) GS 995, at www.churchofengland.org/sites/default/files/2018-01/gs%20misc%20995_July11.pdf

Croft, S. (1999) *Ministry in Three Dimensions*, London: DLT.

Dulles, A. (1987) *Models of the Church*, expanded edition, New York: Doubleday.

Goodhew, D. (ed.) (2015) *Towards a Theology of Church Growth*, Farnham: Ashgate Publishing.

Jackson, B. (2015) *What Makes Churches Grow? Vision and Practice in Effective Mission*, London: Church House Publishing.

Jones, B. (2013) *Mara! Africa Bridges the Gap Between Church and Life*, Aliquid Novum.

McGrath, A. E. (1999) *Reformation Thought: An Introduction*, 3rd edition, Oxford: Blackwell.

Moynagh, M. (2017) *Church in Life: Innovation, Mission and Ecclesiology*, London: SCM Press.

Mung'ong'o, P. L. and Matonya, M. (2013), in *The Wiley-Blackwell Companion to the Anglican Communion Handbook*, ed. I. Markham et al., Oxford: Wiley-Blackwell.

Piroute, L. (1987) *Black Evangelists: The Spread of Christianity in Uganda 1891–1914*, London: Rex Collings.

Potter, P. and Mobsby, I. (2017) *Doorways to the Sacred: Developing Sacramentality in Fresh Expressions of Church*, Norwich: Canterbury Press.

Rowell, G. and Hall, C. (eds) (2004) *The Gestures of God: Explorations in Sacramentality*, London: Continuum.

Sachs, W. L. (2018) 'Introduction', *The Oxford History of Anglicanism*, vol. 5, Oxford: Oxford University Press.

Spencer, N. (2016) *Doing Good: A Future for Christianity in the 21st Century*, London: Theos.

Spencer, S. (2007) *SCM Studyguide: Christian Mission*, London: SCM Press.

US Bishops, *Bishops Guidelines to RCIA*, at, for example: www.true crosschurch.org/documents/Rel%20Ed/Steps%20of%20RCIA.pdf

Walls, A. F. (1996) *The Missionary Movement in Christian History: Studies in the Transmission of Faith*, Maryknoll, NY: Orbis Books.

Wells, S., Rook, R. and Barclay, D. (2017) *For Good: The Church and the Future of Welfare*, Norwich: Canterbury Press.

Woodhead, L. (2015) 'The challenges that the new C of E reports duck', *Church Times*, 23 January.

Index